Shalita's Prayers

*The Remarkable Story of Love, Loss and
One Woman's Unshakable Faith*

Bill Blackburn

All Scripture quotations are taken from the Holy Bible, New International Version®, NIV® Copyright ©1973, 1978, 1984, 2011 by Biblica, Inc.® Used by permission. All rights reserved worldwide.

Book cover design by Jason Hunnicutt, Buzzhive Marketing.

ISBN-13: 978-1719057271
ISBN-10: 1719057273

Printed in the United States of America

First Edition: July 2018

The author may be contacted via email at:
bill.blackburn6@gmail.com

More information at: http://shalitasprayers.com

This book is dedicated to my two amazing sons, Dryw Owens and Daniel Blackburn. Your mother would be very proud of you, as am I.

Contents

Acknowledgments

This book started as a simple writing exercise in 2008 to get my thoughts on paper, never intending for it to be published. But as the writing continued — in part a catharsis for me — and I had the idea of including some of Shalita's journaling, the course changed.

A few individuals provided timely, heartfelt encouragement as I meandered down the long path of developing this book. In particular, thanks go to my sister Susan for her helpful feedback and urging me to continue, as well as my sons, Dryw and Daniel. Thanks as well to Kathy Gibbons, Suzanne Korosec, Lynda Reiner-Leith and Starlene Burgett for their excellent comments, edits and support. Generous thanks also go to Eric Stanford and editor Lori Jones of Edit Resource. Your suggestions and sound guidance were extremely valuable. And to Jason Hunnicutt and Serge Lysak with Buzzhive Marketing – thank you for your outstanding design work and outreach ideas.

I feel a debt of gratitude also to the many people that helped me through the many dark days and frequent stumbles. To Rick Armbruster, Dr. Katherine Bisharat, Carol Voyles, Roselene and Dick Kelley, Clare and Jack Dendinger, Sharon Gordon-Link, Dan Link, Kim and Dave Robertson, Lynn Hutchinson, and the entire Chitambar family (you're awesome!).

Finally, the events, times and people described in the book are based on my best recollections. Any errors or inaccuracies are mine alone.

Introduction

There are moments in life when sometimes all you can do to keep your head above water is to stop and say, "Dear God, I don't know how, but please help me get through this." That moment for me came one December day as I stood by my wife Shalita's hospital bed. Weary from surgery and radiation treatments, suffering for weeks with intense back pain, Shalita had just been diagnosed with a second recurrence of cancer. It was becoming painfully clear that we were near the end.

Feelings of despair welling up in me, I didn't know how I could possibly manage without her, the love of my life. Fearing the future and dreading the worst, all I could do was hang on to my faith, a faith that had welded the two of us together.

Shalita and I met in our early thirties, and though we were married just a dozen years, it seemed like a lifetime. During that time we overcame numerous obstacles, from cultural differences to opposing ideas of parenting. We each suffered the pain of losing a parent. Throughout the challenges, the milestones, and the many celebrations that made up our lives, Shalita and I grew incredibly close.

She was remarkable in so many ways and had an amazing gift with people. She could meet a woman in a class, at church, or even in her room at the hospital and, within minutes, enter her world and make her feel as if they had been friends for years. She took a genuine interest in people and they, more often than not, found her warm, engaging, and very unique.

While we had both grown up in Christian homes and were both the youngest in our families—she had two older brothers and I have an older half brother and two older sisters—we had vastly different upbringings. The son of a state worker and a stay-at-home mom, I grew up in a modest middle class suburb east of Sacramento; Shalita was born in northern India and grew up in a family that was substantially better off than most Indians. Despite our many differences, Shalita and I shared a commitment to God and similar values that became the cornerstone of our marriage. We were deeply in love.

That dreary December day in 2006, she was admitted in the oncology section at Sutter General Hospital in Sacramento, California, where a little more than two years earlier, she had been diagnosed with advanced ovarian cancer and had gone through surgery and brutal rounds of chemotherapy. After more than a year and a half of being cancer free, it had come back with a vengeance. And now the tests showed she had several tumors along her spine, leaving her both physically and emotionally weak. The future was bleak.

A little more than a month after Shalita was admitted into the hospital, she died. In the wrenching days and weeks that followed, as I struggled through my grief, I began to read through her journals, in which she regularly wrote. There were more of them than I had realized—more than a dozen in fact—some dating back to her childhood. Many journals contained old photographs or notes from our boys. There were cards and letters from friends and from admiring students, numerous notes tucked neatly inside. While some journals were only partially filled, others were packed full, each page a small window into her life.

I hadn't realized that her journaling was actually much more than simple descriptions of her days or rants spilling onto the pages. Rather, they were mostly prayers to God, who was even more precious to Shalita than her beloved family. It was through her journals that she poured out her confessions, her requests and fears to the Lord, with honesty and eloquence. Her journals spoke of her intimate relationship with God, and her writings were filled with praises and requests, asking God's blessing and protection for our families and friends. Moreover, within these pages she revealed her hurts and inner struggles to the Lord, constantly showering him with gratitude in both large and small areas of her life.

As I found and read each of her journals, I slowly began to see a more complete picture of my wife, and how her passion for seeking God's direction revealed a deeper level of faith than I had fully realized. Reading her hopes and dreams and prayers caused me to reexamine my own relationship with God, and provided a powerful inspiration for me to dig deeper into the faith we had shared.

Shalita was a gift to many people in her life, and certainly the greatest gift of my life. Through her journals, Shalita gave me a

2

precious, lasting gift that I never knew I needed, but one that has richly blessed me. My hope for this book is that you, too, will be encouraged by these prayers, by her life story and her legacy of a rock-solid faith. I pray that these words lead you into a deeper faith in who God is and what he has planned for you, and that they will lead you to discover the many gifts of your own life.

Teach me Lord to Wait

Here I am in your waiting room Lord –
You do not bid me to move ahead
Nor to go back
Just to sit at your feet and wait
Ah Lord! It's hard –
My heart desires to run ahead
The fact of not knowing hurts.
I want to know – to know and be sure.
Yet you hold me still.
In quietness and confidence shall be my strength.
Wait my daughter in Perfect Faith.
Rest alone in my arms of Grace.
I know your heart
I feel your pain
I care about each loss or gain.
I have great things in store for you
Far beyond your dreams can soar.
Tis' in waiting alone your heart will melt
To yield to me your dreams, hopes and all you felt.
I love you more than you will know
And my blessings on you overflow.
I work in you to fulfill my plan
of making the best woman for your man.
So that through you I may reign on.
As you trust and obey from dusk to dawn.
Yes my Lord I trust in you
I depend on you with all my heart
Belief beyond feeling
Trust beyond situations
My only hope lies in You.
So here I am in your waiting room Lord
With a thankful heart.
Not Knowing
Yet praising
Not seeing
Yet believing

4

Not doing
Just waiting.
In trust
In hope
And
In you.

From Shalita's journal
December 28, 1981

Chapter 1

Growing Up in India

Shalita with her parents in India.

Her name was as exotic as her looks. Born Shalita Tripti Priyamvada Chitambar, she came from a long line of well-educated and successful Indians who migrated north from Bombay (now Mumbai) to the state of Uttar Pradesh (U.P.) during the late nineteenth century.

The Chitambar family has a rich spiritual history. Like most Indians, the early Chitambars were practicing Hindus, but with the influx of Western Christian missionaries in the late nineteenth century, a major shift occurred in the Chitambar family that would influence generations to come. Ultimately, it would plant a seed that established a heritage of faith that became the family's foundation.

Shalita's great-grandfather, Raja Ram Chitambar, was a devoted Hindu. In the 1870s he was a student at Wilson College in

Bombay. One day he bought a copy of the Bible from a man preaching in the bazaar. The young Chitambar reputedly tore it into pieces and mockingly said to the preacher: "Here is your inspired Bible! Let me see what you will do to me!" A short time later he bought a Bible with the intention of finding mistakes and inconsistencies within its pages. But instead of discrediting the Bible, he was struck with a powerful feeling that God wanted to change his heart. He converted to Christianity and decided to be baptized, knowing that this act would cause a great uproar among his relatives and neighbors. As anticipated, much of the family and the community were furious when they heard that he had rejected Hinduism to follow Jesus Christ.

And so, still a boy, Raja Ram left home, traveling north several hundred miles to the city of Allahabad and married at fifteen years old.[1] One of his children from this marriage was Jashwant Rao. Jashwant grew up with a deep commitment to the Christian faith, and became the first Methodist Bishop of India in 1931. Jashwant had eight children; the youngest was John Benedict Chitambar, Shalita's father.

Jashwant traveled several times to the United States and other countries during his ministry, and was asked often about the charismatic new leader of the people who was pushing for Indian independence. It was from these inquiries and from the encouragement of those around him, that Bishop Chitambar published the book *Mahatma Gandhi, His Life, Work and Influence* in 1933.

Bishop Chitambar was well loved and respected. A chapel in Lucknow, the capital of the state of U.P., was named in his honor. Although he died from a heart attack at the relatively young age of 60, his strong faith influenced many, especially his children.

Shalita's parents were both born in Lucknow, while the country was still under British rule. In 1947 they witnessed India win its long-fought-for freedom from her Western oppressor, and the wrenching conflict that followed as the country partitioned into modern-day Pakistan and India.

---

[1] From *The Making of a Bishop: The Life Story of Bishop Jashwant Rao Chitambar* by Brenton Thoburn Badley, published in 1949.

In 1949, Shalita's father—Ben, as he was known—married Thea David. In pursuit of their graduate degrees, they attended Cornell University on scholarships. Thea received her master's degree in psychology and child development. Ben received his Ph.D. in rural sociology, and used this training to help people both in India and, later in life, in various developing regions throughout Asia and Africa. He was also very interested in education and was eventually named president of the Agricultural Institute of Allahabad.[2] Over his lifetime, he published several books on rural sociology.

Chris was the firstborn child of Ben and Thea. Three years later came John; then Shalita six years after John. Like their parents, the Chitambar children were heavily influenced at an early age by hearing Bible stories—an essential part of the fabric of the family. In a country made up mostly of Hindus and Muslims, the Chitambars were in the minority raising their family as Christians, which in some ways made them appreciate the uniqueness of their faith.

I discovered an interesting letter written to Shalita, which highlights the family's spiritual legacy from Bishop Chitambar. The letter, written in the early 1970s, states a key verse often quoted within the family. The letter was from Ben's brother, Ted, which described their father, the Bishop.

Your Grandpa, Shalita, was the most wonderful man who ever lived. His mother died when he was only five, and his father left him an orphan at the age of 14, yet he turned out to be one of the most outstanding men of his time. The secret of his success was that he followed the instructions of his Lord and Master, Jesus Christ, who said: "Seek ye first the kingdom of God and His righteousness, and all these things shall be added unto you." (Mathew 6:33)

Your wonderful grandpa's life was a perfect illustration of this verse. He . . . took as his motto Colossians 1:18 – "That in all

---

[2] The Institute was later renamed the Sam Higginbottom University of Agriculture, Technology and Sciences (SHUATS), after its founder. After his death in 2005, the University created the *Chitamber School of Humanities and Social Sciences* for Dr. Chitambar, but, sadly, misspelled his last name.

things He might have the pre-eminence." And accordingly, he put God first in everything he did . . . We have a wonderful heritage, and may we remain true to the faith of our father and grandfather.

Your ever loving,
Uncle Ted

The Chitambar family did indeed have a wonderful heritage, one of unwavering commitment to following Christ. Just as young Raja Ram Chitambar embraced the faith more than a century before, many of his descendants, now scattered around the world, are committed Christians today.

***

Shalita often said she had an idyllic childhood. She and her brothers grew up on the campus of the Agricultural Institute, which was its own unique, sheltered community. Like most Indians at the time, Shalita and her brothers grew up without television. As a result, one of the main forms of entertainment was reading books, a pleasure Shalita carried into adulthood.

Shalita's mother said that Shalita was a very sensitive girl throughout her childhood, with a great sense of fairness. Although Shalita was named by her brother John, who had given his toy doll the name Shalita—which her parents liked enough to keep—they later found out that in Lebanon, Shalita is the name of a saint. Shalita's closest friend was her neighbor, Nundani, or "Chutku," as she was called. Like Shalita, Chutku's father also worked at the Institute. Whether hanging out or plotting mischief, the two girls were inseparable.

The Chitambar home had servants, as did most well off Indian families. There was a driver, a cook, and someone who cleaned the house and ran errands. Shalita had her "ayah," who, like a nanny, helped her dress and get ready for school each morning. The servants loved little Shalita, whom they called "Rani," or "princess," in Hindi.

From an early age Shalita loved to write. Sometimes even after she was told to turn out the lights and go to sleep, Shalita could be found hiding under the bed sheets, writing with the use of a small lamp. She began keeping a journal when she was about ten. With occasional interruptions, she continued journaling throughout the rest of her life. This early entry, written in 1970, when she was eleven, shows a precocious little girl engaged in self-discovery and offers an interesting glimpse into her priorities and personality. Shalita's writing also sheds light on the tumultuous times.

Who am I? Me. A girl. My parent's youngest and only daughter, Chutku's best friend – Nobody's girl at present.

Sometimes I wish I could really look at myself. I know I'm not perfect. I'm pretty big-mouthed at times, impatient, headstrong and sometimes quite dumb. I can't bear to see anyone or anything in pain. I'm very emotional. I like buying things for other people rather than for myself. I love kids. I'll have about a half a dozen when I get married. I like people – different kinds of them. The human race is so interesting and fascinating. I wonder what impression people get when they see me. Sometimes I just freeze up with certain kinds of people. Some things in this world make me sad – war and poverty are some of them. War is ugly. Why do so many people have to suffer and resort to war – so many lives are lost and most of them are innocent lives? To me the most beautiful words in the world are Peace and Love. Wherever there is peace and love there is joy. Maybe if we started to love each other more – remember that other people have some rights too – maybe the world would be a better place to live in.

I love music. It really turns me on. I find peace in music. When I get mad at a person – I blow up and explode and then it's all over. I can't stay angry at anyone for long. I like to be on good terms with everybody and I don't mind saying 'I'm sorry' to people whom I've hurt. When I get mad I like to be alone.

There are times when I treasure my own company – I like to be alone and think. I just take aimless walks to nowhere to be by myself – to dream and build fantasy castles in the air.

When I fall in love – it'll be with only one special guy and I'll get married to the same guy. I believe marriage is for keeps. I'd love to be a housewife – stay at home – centre my life around my husband and children.

Who am I? For one thing, almost a woman.

Even at this early age, this entry says a lot about Shalita's temperament and her developing attitudes in life. Shalita's fascination with "different kinds of people" was certainly influenced by her father's position as president of the Allahabad Institute, which routinely hosted missionaries, dignitaries, and other visitors from around the world. Her love of children would continue, eventually leading her to a master's degree in human development and working at a daycare center prior to her work as a college professor. Shalita's fondness for giving gifts also continued throughout her life.

Like her parents and brothers, Shalita was tall, especially for an Indian girl. She said that she sometimes felt self-conscious about it and was occasionally teased about being chubby before she lost her pre-adolescent baby fat. She blossomed into a tall, trim, and striking young woman.

This diary is being written on June 1st 1974 on the eve of Chutku's going away. We are in my bedroom on my bed and are reliving those 15 golden years of our beautiful friendship.

"MEMORIES"
By: Shalita Chitambar & Chutku Das

October 1957 saw Sulakshana Nandini (Chutku) Das step into this world. And on May 1959, Shalita Tripti Priyamvada Chitambar arrived.

We don't remember how we met – we just 'happened.' Our earliest memories date back to days of the dolls. We had Julie and Flower Ken, who were our favourite dolls. We would spend hours, bathing, dressing, feeding and taking them for pram-rides.

Once we even oiled their hair with 'Jabakusum,' which we used to call 'Jaikuslum.' We used to fill the bathing tub with water and 'swim' in it. Being the youngest of both families we were usually left out of games. Once while the rest of the gang were playing on our lawn and Chutku and I were left to our own devices on how to amuse ourselves, we plucked off all of Mum's prize lilies, leaving not a single one and laboriously arranged them on a little hedge surrounding our flower bed. We were waiting to be duly thanked for our pains when that creep Transie Singh let the cat out of the bag and we were thoroughly spanked by both our mummies, which was a perfect ending for a perfect day!!

. . . The cooler had a great attraction for us. We used to stand in front of it draped in a sari and would sing the national anthem.

. . . We both went to St. Mary's Covenant School and even tho' Chuts was 2 years my senior we spent all our free time together, and as tho' that wasn't enuff we even made the preposterous excuse of returning a pencil barely an inch long just to 'visit' each other during class hours. The best part was when we both won the Essay competition prize together – we both had and still have an aptitude for essay writing. Miss Violet Lyons was our favourite teacher who taught us when each of us was in std. III.

. . . It seemed like our big moments occurred simultaneously, like when we both garlanded Indira Gandhi [the Prime Minister] when she visited the Institute.

. . . Like all close friends we did have our tiffs but they were only momentary and only helped to bring us even closer.

Pinkie, our bitterest enemy, did her best to try to break up our friendship, but never succeeded with her turned-down corner mouth. She was the most unpleasant <u>BITCH</u> and always left a bad taste in our mouths. She was the bone of contention, we actively loathed her. We even overcame the insurmountable difficulty in learning cycling. Once Chuts learnt she taught me and we were soon pedaling our way thru the countryside. We formed a club called the "Mystic Myths" with the 2 of us as its sole members. Our password was "PICKLED TOES."

In 1967 the floods attacked the AAI [Allahabad Agricultural Institute] and it was fun for Chuts and me but not for other members in our family as our house is situated right near the river. It proved to be quite an exhilarating experience as we paddled over our water covered lawn on boats to each other's houses. The most repugnant sight was having slimy snakes swimming all over the place. We even went boating over our hedge, which was quite an unusual spectacle. The Fosters – an American family – came during the thick of it to the Institute. After the floods receded it was a big job resuming the normal schedule.

When Shalita's brother Chris went away to college to begin his study of medicine she missed him terribly, but in the process she grew closer to John. And when Chris fell in love with Deb, a bright, bubbly college girl from Iowa visiting India on an exchange program, Shalita looked up to her as the big sister she never had.

Deb recounted a few stories of Shalita's childhood, including a visit she made to see them when Chris was in medical school. The two were soul sisters from the very beginning. They first met when Shalita was eleven years old, and became pen pals after Deb returned to college in Minnesota. Deb also shared that one of Shalita's letters eagerly informed her of the plans she was making for the upcoming wedding of Barbie and Ken. Shalita was busy making decorations from paper and designs from cloth.

After Chris and Deb were married in Allahabad in late 1973, they moved to Ludhiana, about six hundred miles northwest where Chris started medical school. When they made it home to visit family at the Institute, Shalita anxiously awaited their arrival and greeted them excitedly "with sparkling eyes and a smile that lit up the room." Soon the guitar came out, and they would sing their favorite Beatles and Elton John tunes. Deb and Shalita developed a special relationship. The two got along extremely well and their closeness continued over the years.

The fact that Shalita was a sound sleeper was revealed to Deb one night when she was visiting them in their tiny apartment at the Christian Medical College. Deb tells the story: "Our bedroom was also our living room, dining room, and study. We had a hand-made double bed that took up a good share of the room. The charpai (portable bed) that we had borrowed for Shalita needed to be returned to its owner, who unexpectedly returned from a trip in the middle of the night. There was only one place left for Shalita to sleep, and that was in the bed with Chris and me. After considerable adjusting to get the three of us comfortable, we all managed to fall asleep. Jolted awake, I heard a thud followed by silence. I put on my glasses to see what had happened. There, on the hard concrete floor, lay Shalita, still soundly asleep. Fearing she had hurt her head, I tapped her shoulder and asked, 'Are you ok?' 'What happened?' Shalita replied. By then Chris had woken up, and we jumped up to investigate. Shalita seemed surprised and reported that she felt no pain. We checked her out, all was well, and we breathed a sigh of relief. The next morning we remarked how lucky we were that our three-in-a-bed routine culminated in a funny story, with no injuries!"

Shalita was also extremely close to both of her parents. She said to me more than once that the love and security she felt from her own father made it easier for her to understand our Heavenly Father's love and protection. At sixteen, Shalita made a personal commitment to follow Jesus Christ. It was an earnest and heartfelt commitment, much like my own personal decision at age fourteen. Even though she had been brought up in a Christian family and had believed in God, her personal commitment as a teen was pivotal. As a young Christian, she threw herself into Bible studies and became very involved in music in the church.

One of the ways she praised God and expressed her feelings was through journaling, acknowledging the Creator and often lavishing praises on the Lord. At nineteen, Shalita was in Burma traveling with her parents, and made this entry in the "traditional church" style she grew up with.

June 14, 1978
Lord, I'm sitting out here in the verandah just reflecting on the beauty around me, which thou hast created. Only a beautiful God can create such beauty and Lord how beautiful thou art – I see thee in everything around me – Thy hands have created all these wonders and I worship Thee. I feel Thee in thy cool breeze, which caresses my skin – which soothes me and calms me – which refreshes me and restores me – the breeze of thy love – of Thee. I see Thee in the blue hills in front of me – when I lift up mine eyes to the hills. I know that thou art my help and my strength – my keeper and guardian – I see Thee in the soft sighing of the trees – the shade and comfort I feel under the security of thy branches – I see Thee in the swaying of the grass – I look above and see the boundless expanse of the blue sky – dotted with clouds like puffs of cottonwool. I learn so much from Thee by just gazing at the sky and clouds – Behind the dark clouds of my sorrow – my grief and hard times – is the glorious endless expanse of thy self – How wonderful it is to know dear Lord that the blue of heaven is greater than the sky.

And as I sit here and meditate reminded of my own insignificance and inadequacy in this world – I am but a pebble – but Lord use this pebble to build up your house – smooth out its rough edges. Wash away its dirt and let it shine for Thee. Thou who didst create this big beautiful and wonderful earth – accept me in my weakness – in my wretchedness and make me what you will my Savior. I am Thine!

***

Like her brothers, Shalita attended the Agricultural Institute, the campus she had grown up on. She shared that it was difficult being the president's daughter, and felt the pressure to both excel in her academics and be cognizant of how she behaved around campus. It was especially uncomfortable at times since they lived on campus. And, like her brothers, she did extremely well in school.

When she completed her bachelor's degree at the Institute, she decided to seek a master's degree in home economics at the Maharaja Sayajirao University of Baroda, about eight hundred miles southwest of her home. Being the youngest and so close to her parents, it was a difficult transition being away from home. The distance brought out feelings she hadn't ever experienced, and she began questioning whether she had made a mistake leaving home. It was a difficult time, but one that brought much personal growth.

July 16, 1979, Baroda

The ache of loneliness is too painful for me to bear. My tears wet my pillow – they brim from my heart as from a fathomless pool. Help me Lord – Fill this emptiness – ease my homesickness. Thy ways are so hard to understand. Thy thoughts are far above Thine. Teach me to bear suffering as thy soldier. Dry my tears – ease my longing – my ache for Dad and Mum and home – Please Lord. I don't know why you've brought me here. I don't like being so far from home. I don't want to come back next semester. I want to be at home with Dad and Mum. I hate the hostel food – oh Lord – you understand. I feel so lost here, it's so huge, overwhelming and I feel so inadequate. Ease the fears – will I be able to come up to the mark? It's so different, so impersonal.

I am 20 years old and yet I feel a little girl – I want to run into my Dad's arms and feel protected. I want to feel my Mummy's arms around me and her hands soothing my face. Lord, I can't take this anymore. I want to go home. Why is this separation so painful, Lord? I want to feel the security and familiarity of home's loved ones – Yet Lord – I know that my security lies in Thee and in trusting you. I love you and want your will done. That's why I've come here. So please help me. Please heal my ache, fill me with your peace and love. Let these days pass quickly – really quickly so I can be home soon in October. Just 3 months left. Yes, it will pass fast and soon I will be home again.

Surround my beloved and precious parents with the assurance and comfort of your presence. Fill them with yourself. Thank you for them. Be with Chris and Deb and Christine. Release thy spirit and let it overflow in their lives. Bless my... [brother] John. Continue to guide him and enable him to keep on trusting you.

Lord, don't let these tears be of self-pity. Take them away. Nurture the seed thou has sown in me. Make me fruitful here. Use me, teach me thru these tears, even though it's so painful being away from home. Thank you for the ache of separation, for all the tears for I know that only thru these you are going to mould me, shape me and make me into the woman you want me to be. Help me put away childish things and walk as thy woman – mature in body, mind and spirit – as I forget myself and learn to be concerned about others. I love you.

December 15, 1979
Thank you Lord for bringing me to Baroda – for healing me in my loneliness and tears and showing me again and again each day what a Great and Loving Lord you are. I have matured so much since I've come here and I know that you have brought me here. It has been painful in the initial adjustment but your grace has made me stronger.

Despite the initial loneliness she felt being away at college, her time in Baroda was pivotal for her educational and emotional development. Just before Shalita moved to the US, she wrote this lovely prayer poem.

June 15, 1981
Teach me Lord today I pray
To look beyond the rain of afflictions
To the rainbow and sunshine of your promises.
Teach me not to live in the here and now

Entrapped by my focus on the grey bleakness
But give me a vision to pause for you
What you are making me to be –
A channel of love – of compassion,
Patience and tenderness
Are the showers needed to flourish these
Flowers too painful for me to bear?
Is it too hard for me to look beyond these
Showers to the flowers?
Nurturing showers are not always pleasant
Nor do the harsh words always soothe me
But I know that my Redeemer liveth
I know that He works and plans for good
Because I am His cherished vine.
He works in me right here and now
Through showers and storm, hail and fire
Yes Lord, it's raining hard for me right now
Much I do not understand
Yet this I know that you know best
And care to let me trust and rest
Showers of blessing I praise you for these
Dark gray showers fringed with gold
Luminous, flooding, blinding showers
Yet nurturing and budding little flowers
Making me fertile, pliant and ripe
Till the full harvest of life is reaped
Here I am Lord waiting for you
Let me blossom and flourish all that you sow
For I truly realize now more than anything else
That through this rain and through this storm
The most beautiful thing you want me to be is me.

Chapter 2

'Coming to USA'

When Shalita's brother Chris fell in love with Deb, the seeds were planted for the family's eventual move to the United States. Chris finished medical school in India in 1976, and he and Deb moved to the US to complete his residency. A few years later her brother John left home to pursue his Ph.D. in nematology at the University of California at Davis. It wasn't long before the rest of the family eventually followed to California. As Shalita finished up her master's degree in child development and home economics from the university in Baroda, she decided to pursue another master's, this time in human development, also at UC Davis.

In early 1981, Shalita and her parents flew together to California. Shalita's father took on a new role as Director of Community Development in developing countries with World Vision, a Christian non-profit organization. It was a big change for her father in particular, leaving academia for the field, quite literally, as he used his expertise in rural sociology and traveled extensively to developing countries. Although not planned, the move to the US became permanent for all the Chitambars. While her parents settled in the southern California suburb of Arcadia, Shalita was four hundred miles north in Davis, just west of Sacramento.

October 15, 1981, Davis, California
Here I am in USA Lord and wherever I am – I am with you, never ever separated from the height, depth and breadth of your great glorious and perfect love. How deeply I love you Father – my own precious and blessed Jesus – with all the fibre and intensity of my being. I want to shout out and sing your faithfulness to me. Morning by morning new mercies I see – All I have needed your hand has provided – Great is your faithfulness to me. Thank you for bringing me to Davis –

for caring for each detail. It is truly a miracle and I know that in being at Davis I am truly in the centre of your will.

Dear Lord my heart is so full – you know my thoughts before I even think them or verbalize them in prayer and you love, honour and respect my desires. Father I come before you as a child – leaning and trusting so totally on you.

Shalita initially moved in with John in Davis, making her transition a little easier. While Shalita had lived for a year in Madison, Wisconsin, and although English was her first language, she said it was nonetheless a difficult transition. She felt like an outsider, in part because few people knew much about Indians when she arrived.

February 6, 1982
Thank you Lord for times of breaking. For times of building. For times of shaping and showing me how precious I am to you. Thank you Lord for me – Just me – as I am with my strengths, vulnerabilities and insecurities. Thank you for making me the most beautiful person in your eyes (only by your grace) for the day I was conceived Lord – you knew it all and planned me – chose me and love me the way I am. Thank you for in your sight there is only one Shalita Chitambar and she is very precious to you. You have graven her name in the palms of your hand and you will never let her slip away from you. Lord, I'm glad to be me. I love you with all the fibre and intensity of my life.

Lord I claim the above with faith and trust. It's a new beginning – this realization of myself in you and you in me and I love you.

While Shalita's parents lived a good distance away in Southern California, she remained in close contact and visited them often. This letter from her dad while he was traveling is evidence of their special relationship. Further, it shows the important legacy of what he considered most essential in life.

November 10, 1985

Beloved Shalita,

Yesterday I was in Narita and as I walked along a familiar path from Narita station down the narrow street lined with interesting shops my thoughts went back three years when a sweet, excited and eager girl walked with me as we looked into a few shops, nibbled on yakitori, almost bought chestnuts and went down almost to the bottom of the street to see the Japanese temple! All the while Ma took her time in a few shops and we rushed back to have lunch together in a small restaurant. Then the rush to catch the bus back to the airport hotel, putting things together, finding my watch and finally checking in at the airport to complete the last lap of our journey to San Francisco. Do you remember? It all came back as a happy treasured memory that will always remain along with other memories of joys, pain and happiness and closeness as you, our youngest, grew up and "this girl became a woman." Each one of you in a special way has a special place and you, beloved Shalita, our daughter, a _very_ special place and we thank God for all you mean to us. And so, while I really did not do much in Narita it was a sentimental journey as I looked and walked and thought and remembered.

No man could be blessed more in a daughter than the blessing and joy and comfort that you have brought me. God bless you my little girl and keep you in His care. Never forget who and what you are and the heritage that is yours. God has given you much in material things – never forget the priorities and values that you have been brought up to cherish.

Remain always the sweet, simple girl that you have been with the beauty of Jesus shining through you darling, for all the happy memories and the love that you give to Ma and to me – Such beautiful memories, Narita is just one of them. This is just a little old note from little old me. Am getting over jet lag after the flight from Tokyo to Sura in Fiji. Look in your map and find me. I am truly in the South Pacific.

23

Love and miss you much.
Much love forever, your devoted Dad.

***

As Shalita acclimated to her new life in Northern California, she plunged into her studies at UC Davis. It was during this time as a grad student that she met another student there. His name was Mark. They dated for several months. It was Shalita's first significant long-term relationship. When Mark wanted to get married, despite some objections from her family, Shalita was happy to oblige. They were married in late 1983.

For Shalita, it was an answer to prayer and a wish come true, as she had longed to be married and raise a family. In early 1986 Shalita became pregnant, giving birth to Dryw that October. In what became a book of letters to Dryw, she shared her excitement of being his mother.

January 3, 1987
I will never forget how I felt when I first found out I was pregnant – excitement, confusion, apprehension – Can this really be happening to me? My child within is truly a miracle. I felt sure all along this child in me was a boy. I dreamed about him – talked to him and loved him. He was flesh of my flesh – my body was no longer mine. I first felt him kick me at 3 1/2 months – a tiny flutter – I was awed. This was a life in me – moving. When I saw him on the screen during my ultrasound he was waving his arms up and down. "That's quite a gymnast you have in there," the technician said.

I cried seeing my child. Physically I felt good during my pregnancy, except for nausea and backache. Everyone said I looked great. Emotionally I was in a traumatic state. My world around me was falling apart. It wasn't how I wanted it . . . Truly my child is a survivor. I feel such a unique bond with him because we went through so much together – How I love you my own baby.

At 1:20 a.m. our precious son Dryw Dylan was born – I am a mother – How saturated I am with love for you my own precious Dryw! You were worth every tear I shed – all the pain I bore – my gift. When I first saw you I couldn't believe the incredible joy in me. You have awakened in us your parents hope for our future – a love for each other that we felt dying – we see in you our love – our life anew.

My precious Dryw – no mother ever loved her son as much as I love you – I would die for you – I want only the best for you – To make a home where there is peace, laughter and security, which comes from Jesus.

Dryw my son – you are a very special and cherished boy – a chosen one – God has great plans for you. He loves you even more than I do – What an incredible thought!

What a beautiful baby you are! I feel so proud that you formed so perfectly in me. You are truly a miracle of God – so healthy and beautiful. You have big hands – always use them to serve God and to do good to others – large brown eyes – long fingers. Eyebrows like your Dad – You are a gorgeous color – Oh Dryw you are lovely. I was on such a high after you were born – I felt like I had really accomplished something. God had kept his promise to me in Psalms 91 "No harm had befallen my tent." Thank you Jesus!

January 24, 1987
How wonderful it was when you slept through the night! That was your Christmas present to me, and yet I found that I missed that 3 am feeding. Holding you – how I enjoyed that quiet time. It was as though there was no one else in the world but you and me. My heart bursts with love for you – You are smiling so much now! I just melt whenever you do. You've also started following me with your eyes.

You give me a special look that tells me that you know that I'm your mama. Whenever I nurse you I feel such a deep unbreakable bond. You clutch at me and I look down at you just flooding with love – You have added such a new and wonderful dimension to my life.

February 28, 1987
Dryw – you light up my life – You started smiling and laughing this month and I just dissolve – Your whole body smiles! You are such a happy baby. I love the way you lift your eyebrows and smile with your eyes – You are so alert and intelligent! You love to smile at people – especially girls – You little flirt!! I weaned you from the breast at 4 months. I miss it but we were both ready for it!

July 17, 1987
You are almost 9 months old my precious baby – what a big boy you are!! I look at you and marvel at how perfectly formed you are – you've started tightening your arms around my neck whenever I pick you up – You are such a love! I love snuggling with you, kissing your fat little legs, arms, tummy and cheeks – You also say "Mama." Dryw – when you read this know how much I love you – you are the most important person in my life – You are my sunshine – You will never know how much of a reason you gave me for carrying on when I didn't feel like living – I want only what's best for you my precious son … I am astonished at how intense and fierce my love is for you – I want to protect you. Dryw whatever happens always know I love you more than my own life.

While Shalita loved becoming a mother her marriage with Mark became a bitter struggle. Shalita had once told me that her marriage was fraught with conflict and division after its first year. They battled well before Dryw was born, and Shalita ached over their relationship, but did her best to try to make the marriage work.

This card Shalita sent to her dad, whom she sometimes lovingly called "Binki," typifies her affection towards him and showed his counsel as she and Mark struggled in marriage.

My Beloved and Sweet Binki,

Just wanted you to know that I am praying very specially for you and that you are so close in my love and prayers. You are so precious to me my Dad – more than you'll ever know. Please take care of yourself and be a good steward of your health. I think much of everything you talked about – your work and yourself. You are a true man of God – Like David you are a man after God's own heart. Always know that Dad. I am so blessed to be your daughter and so proud of you. God has exciting things ahead for you and 1986 will be a wonderful year for us all with Jesus at the helm of our ship.

Dad, God really spoke to Mark and me through what you shared at breakfast with us before we left. "…That in all things Christ might have the preeminence." We have made that our banner for 1986 – both in our marriage and in our individual walk with the Lord. Thank you for sharing that with us.

God bless you with the Light of His love, guidance and wisdom always. You are truly everything your name means Dad – Benedict – our blessing and our benediction given by God to us and to me your own daughter.

I love you with all my heart Dad.

Your girlie,
Shalita

The marriage continued to struggle. Mark was uncomfortable with the amount of time Shalita spent calling and visiting her family, so she pulled back. Constantly worried about her marriage and feeling isolated from her family and friends, it was one of the lowest times in her life.

May 26, 1989
Who would have thought that there could be such sadness and

pain in such a short capsule of time? The Mark I married is no more. I see glimpses of him and I find myself with a stranger who curses God and completely denies Him. My heart is so heavy – Jesus you have always been my reason for living. All I have ever wanted was to serve you and walk in your will. It is so hard to live with someone who has rejected you. Everything I cherish and value is ridiculed – and yet I must continue believing that you will work in Mark and bring him back to yourself. You are the cement of my life – please be the cement of my marriage. Lord I love Mark so much – in spite and despite. I know you will bring him back to you. Only you can soften his heart. You desire it and love him more than I ever can. You are so real God – you are truth and absolute – thank you for being the one constant, never changing factor in my life.

As the relationship deteriorated, Mark developed relationships outside of marriage, destroying any chance of a future together. Shalita was devastated. They divorced in 1990. It was especially painful to Shalita, coming from a family that had had little exposure to divorce. Shalita threw herself into caring for Dryw, who was three and a half at the time. She was starting over.

Shattered
June 17, 1990
If I were to describe what my life has been like this past year or so I would say that it has been a major renovation project.

It's like moving into a house that seems so nice and cozy and then you discover that the roof leaks – When it rains it's cold and wet and when it's dark outside the darkness seeps inside the house too. And I with all my might try to patch that hole in the roof – the patch seems to hold till the next time it rains and then it's cold and wet and I'm frightened of the darkness around me. And the harder I try to patch the hole the bigger it gets. I pray, dear Lord, please fill this hole. Keep the rain out so I can stay dry and warm. And the Lord says – "That's not what I'm going to do – it's not enough to patch the hole – I'm going to build a new house." "Dear Lord," I cry, "why? All I want is for the roof not to leak," and God says, "Let me rebuild your house."

And so it starts – except that rebuilding involves first tearing down the existing structure – it means stripping the plaster and sanding wood – putting in new fixtures, hammering, pounding and scraping. And all the while I keep telling God – "Lord, this is so messy – this hurts so much, it hurts to have the plaster stripped – it hurts to have my edges sanded – all I wanted was a new roof and what are you doing? When will this end? This wasn't what I had in mind."

And gradually through all the dust – the pounding and scraping I begin to see something beautiful emerge. I see a door where there was once a wall – a bay window where there once a tiny skylight – and I say: "Yes Lord, if you hadn't broken it down, this wouldn't be here."

And God in His infinite wisdom smiles. "My child, this is my gift to you – your joy is my joy. Live in this house – enlarge the place of your tent – live for me, for I have only just begun my work in YOU!"

Shalita's time being single again was painful, but, as is often the case, it was also a time of great introspection, adjustment, and personal and spiritual growth. She used the time to examine her life and set personal goals, seeking to draw closer to God.

(About 1990)

Thank you Lord for breaking me – and not just leaving me broken, but for rebuilding me. How I love you. I marvel at how totally AWESOME in every sense of the word you really are. The step of faith I took in receiving you way back in 1975 was only the beginning. Life has been a struggle – it's been up and down, and yet I look back now and see how you have

29

worked. There were times when you felt so far away from me. There were times I felt so completely alone – unloved and unworthy. And yet now I look back and realize that you were probably never closer to me than you were in the moments that I thought you were the farthest. You have worked so incredibly in my life. Tomorrow I will be sharing my testimony in church and I don't want to stand up and let people hear about Shalita's life – but I want them to hear about what YOU can do. How you work – how you break and build up and how you never give up on us. How faithful your love is. Lord you can only use us as long as we are broken before you, so please search my heart right now. Take away anything from me that is not of you and let your Holy Spirit breathe in me. Inspire me – empower me and speak thru me. Let every word that comes out of my mouth glorify you tomorrow morning. Let your Spirit touch hearts – move lives. Be in control of the entire service Lord. Please give me the words to focus on. Fill me Lord Jesus – I need you with every breath I draw – please fill me and touch me.

Bodega Bay
June 23 (probably 1992)
Lord, I have seen such incredible beauty today – the roaring ocean, jagged cliffs, wildflowers. I have heard the sound of seagulls and waves – smelt the salt and felt the breeze and tasted the salt air. You are truly majestic and the greatest artist of all. I have seen the detail you put in nature – from the tiniest wildflower to the roaring sea. I praise you because you are a God of perfection – Everything you create is so lovely for you are altogether lovely.

This trip has been hard for me emotionally – I'm surrounded by memories and am conscious of a deep ache and longing within me. I long for someone to love me. Just for who I am – someone to hold me and care for me – and not just anyone, but the one you have chosen for me, Lord. It's been so long since I have been loved as a woman should be – as you would have me be loved. I have given so much love and I long to receive some from the one you have chosen – who is he Lord? I trust you to bring all things to pass in your time. Please keep my eyes on you. Keep my focus broad. I am afraid to place all my hopes on one person as I am afraid of rejection. Please guide me here Lord. Let your will be made perfect in me Lord.

P.S. Bless him too and prepare his heart for me – whoever he is and wherever he is.

Chapter 3

We Meet

As Shalita began to rebuild her life after her marriage had painfully ended, she sought a full-time job. In the spring of 1990 she was hired as a faculty member at Sierra College, a community college in the fast-growing city of Rocklin, at the base of the Sierra Nevada foothills. She was thrilled to be taken on full time at Sierra, where she taught courses on human development, marriage and family, and related subjects for the Family and Consumer Sciences Department.

The new position allowed Shalita to buy a modest house in Rocklin in May 1990. During the next few years she began to stretch her wings and, when not working or taking care of Dryw, she became very involved in a nearby church and began to lead Bible studies for college students. It was a time of healing and growth.

January 10, 1993
The last time I kept a daily journal I was 18 years old. Over the years I have continued to keep writing and recording my thoughts though not consistently and in one journal. Many of my thoughts have been anguished prayers to God recorded on random pieces of paper – desperate pleas of faith, fits of rage, healing, praise and hopes. I have saved each prayer and have seen the pattern of my life emerge through them and most of all seen God's guidance and leadership in my life.

What format shall this journal take? Should I keep a daily record of my life for all posterity or shall I use this as a catharsis to my emotions, dreams and prayers? Whatever format it may take it shall reflect my total honesty with myself and with God. I am 33 years old – the mother of a precious 6 year-old boy who gives my life joy, fulfillment and purpose. I am single again – the survivor of betrayal, rejection and torment. I am most importantly a woman chosen by God and loved so much by Him. This defines me and must continue to be my complete identity. At this stage in my life, I want so much to be able to see myself through God's eyes – with compassion, love and new every morning – There is so much I crave within my spirit. I crave to be filled with his spirit – to live obediently and joyfully for Him. I want a powerful prayer life, a disciplined heart. I crave the holiness and purity of Jesus in my heart.

I am aware even as I write this, that my hunger for God surpasses my hunger and desire to be loved by a man of God. I have learned that things and affections of this world are fragile and inconsistent. God's love and His power is the only thing worth living for.

I am excited about another year. 1992 was a rough one for me and I'm thankful it's behind me. God, I pray so much that my hunger for you will drive me closer to you. This year please teach me Your perspective in life – in my relationships with others – with myself. Give me your eyes – your spirit. I love you with all my heart. Teach me to put myself on the line for you. I am excited by the challenges ahead. A new semester at school starts next week. I will need grace…

Shalita and I met by chance on a cool morning in December 1992. I was waiting for a friend after the service at Fair Oaks Presbyterian Church. I was standing by a doorway of a classroom when Shalita walked up, looking for a class that was to be held there. "It's cancelled," I said. "There wasn't enough interest." I could see a faint look of disappointment in her dark brown eyes. "That's too bad," she replied. She quietly disappeared and I continued waiting for my friend. She looked familiar to me, and realized that I had seen her before at some Christian singles' events at the church. It was the briefest encounter, quite unremarkable.

Two months later I was having dinner with a friend, Mark Janzen. As we finished the meal Mark mentioned that he was going to meet some friends and listen to jazz at the Sacramento Inn and invited me along. When we arrived he introduced me to his friends, and before I knew it, I was sitting next to a beautiful, exotic-looking woman in a long black dress. I realized that we had met a few months earlier. I introduced myself and she said, "I'm Shalita." "That's a lovely name," I returned. Before long we fell into a lengthy conversation. I don't recall what we talked about, but I remember being impressed that she was very bright and easy to talk with.

At some point I got up to use the restroom, and when I returned, I was disappointed to see another man now occupied my seat. I wanted to continue talking with Shalita, but didn't see an easy way to reinsert myself. I was also very tired, so I told Mark that I was leaving and asked what her name was again. I knew it was an unusual name and was determined to remember it. Under my breath I said her name several times, "Sha-li-ta. Sha-li-ta." I was smitten.

A few nights later I called Shalita and asked if she was interested in going to a concert. "Sure, that sounds fun," she replied. Our first date was set. Since I didn't know her well, I picked a concert at a local church, thinking a casual first date would be best. On Friday, March 12, 1993, and I drove twenty miles from my condo in the north part of Sacramento to Rocklin. As I approached her nicely kept house, I felt that twinge of nervousness in my stomach. I rang the doorbell and took a deep breath.

"Hi! come on in," she said with a warm smile. The house was small but homey. As she disappeared to finish getting ready, I smiled as I heard the sound of one of my favorite instrumental artists, George Winston, playing softly in the background. We left the house and climbed into my silver Oldsmobile. We chatted casually on the way to the concert. I remember driving down the freeway and her commenting about the year she was born and that we must be the same age. She also mentioned she had a six-year-old son. I was a little surprised that she had a child and wondered what he was like.

The concert was for the Christian singer Bruce Carroll. We both enjoyed the concert and felt very comfortable with each other. I remember her making a joke when the offering was taken. One of the pastors of the church made an impassioned plea to give generously. "If they didn't collect enough, God is going to call him home," she said, a reference to a bizarre comment that televangelist Oral Roberts had made some time back. We both laughed. After the concert we went out for an evening snack at Lyon's, a nearby casual restaurant. Worried about making a good impression, Shalita ordered something modest, a muffin and coffee. I, on the other hand, ordered a waffle with whipped cream and strawberry sauce. She teased me about it later, saying she had wanted to order that too.

We continued talking and found we had much in common— she was the youngest child and had two older brothers. I was also the youngest in my family and had two older sisters and a half brother. Our first date was a lot of fun and I knew that I wanted to get to her know her better. I felt a great sense of peace about our budding relationship. I had never met someone like Shalita, and it didn't take long before I felt that there was something really special about her. I thought, *This feels different.* After talking with her that first evening at the Sacramento Inn, I found her to be interesting and very bright, and we enjoyed making each other laugh. And she was stunning. Shalita's beauty stemmed from classic good looks, high cheekbones, a lovely smile and a tall, thin figure. She had beautiful skin and dark, penetrating eyes and black hair. I found her charm, combined with her beauty, engaging—even a little hypnotizing.

One of the qualities that was especially attractive about her was that her faith in God was authentic, without being narrow minded. I had met too many women that had shallow views of the world. Some were strong in their faith, but had rigid views. Shalita possessed a broader view of the world. Growing up in India and traveling extensively to both developed and underdeveloped countries gave her a perspective I had rarely encountered.

I saw Shalita as a potential wife within the first few weeks of knowing her, something I had never felt that quickly or strongly. And while in many ways she was different than anyone I had met, there was something reassuringly familiar about her, something that made being with her very comfortable from the beginning. She possessed an elegant confidence, and yet there was a touch of vulnerability under the surface. It was quickly clear to us both that we shared a similar commitment to our faith, which was foundational to our relationship.

From my journal

March 13, 1993
Two weeks ago a friend of mine, Mark, invited me to dinner and we went to the Sacramento Inn afterwards to listen to some jazz. I talked with a woman I met a few months ago at

Fair Oaks Presbyterian Church. Her name is Shalita. We really hit it off and a few days later I called her to ask her to see Bruce Carroll at Arcade Baptist church… She seems very nice, easy to talk with. And I was amazed how we shared so many of the same views. Wow, what a neat lady!

April 21, 1993
I've been falling lately. Shalita has completely touched me. Sunday after showing slides from my trip to Scotland and dinner at Bert Gaston's we walked through her quiet Rocklin neighborhood. She walked close as the cold was wrapping around us. I seized the opportunity to have her place her arm around mine. She was a most willing companion. I held her hand and another layer of my heart was peeled back and exposed.

She is a truly, truly, truly unique lady. Kind, gentle, strong, warm, timid, graceful. I will see her tomorrow evening here for dinner – it's a very nice feeling inside. ☺

April 22, 1993
We kissed, talked, enjoyed each other. It was heavenly. She is a doll, which, despite not feeling well, made today a <u>very nice day</u>.

April 24, 1993
Where do I start? The feelings I have for Shalita are profound. We talked at length last night on the telephone. We seem to be feeling the same kinds of emotions and desiring the same kind of healthy, God-centered relationship. Just thinking about her can bring my eyes to tears.

I don't remember ever feeling quite like this . . . my first romance, I recall brought out very deep felt emotions, but part of that was because she <u>was</u> my first important relationship. Perhaps the strings of my heart are so tenderly touched because I look at Shalita as a future wife. It's amazing. We still have a lot to learn about each other, but it certainly has captured my attention.

I could listen to Kenny G's Breathless album and dream of her all day, all night. I can't believe the tears . . .

It feels – this is it.

From Shalita's journal

March 11, 1993
. . . I am sensing the beginning of a new friendship with Bill. We met 2 weeks ago. Actually earlier in Dec. and I've seen him around a lot. Had a really nice conversation when we met. He seems very decent and refreshingly balanced. He called me up and asked me out and we're going out tomorrow. I have been praying about this every day. God, please let this friendship grow in the direction and to the intent You want it to grow.

I am excited and also a little nervous. I have met so many jerks and am excited but a little scared. What if he turns out to be just like the others? Please dear Lord, let this one be functional and mature. I have dealt with so much dysfunction around me this week. It seems functional!! Please bless our time together tomorrow night. Let there be laughter and depth, fun and seriousness, sharing and listening and above all dear Father, be pleased and glorified through us. I am only taking it as an evening out and I pray for a friendship to be built founded on you. Help us to be totally relaxed – take away the awkwardness, fumbling and let the evening truly flow. Jesus I love you with all the fiber of my heart. Father, I also pray that my having been married will not frighten him – if it does, it will be a red flag. Please Father, be glorified. I give tomorrow evening to you.

March 13

Thank you Blessed Father for last night. You really answered my prayers. It was such a relaxed and enjoyable feeling and evening and I really feel I have made a new friend. It was so wonderful to talk with a person of spiritual maturity and depth and it was almost scary how much we agreed on issues. Lord Jesus I am not placing any expectation or feeling on last night. Whatever happens is completely in your hands and I trust you. Please keep my focus broad and yet fixed on you. I praise you again for last evening. It was a blessing.

April 22

My heart is so full of peace, excitement and contentment and most of all praise to you father. Bill held me and kissed me tonight and I thought I would melt and float away. He is so tender... so gentle, sweet and sensitive. Father he is so special and I want us to grow together in your love – with each other and you. Please direct our steps. I don't want to rush but want to savor this and see your hand working. This feels so right – Please continue to affirm this in my heart . . . in Bill's and in the hearts of others.

April 26

My cup runneth over . . . with praises and thanksgiving for Your gift of love – for answered prayers – Great is your faithfulness Father – None of my prayers have been unheard or unanswered! Your timing is perfect and you are an awesome God. I am falling deeper in love with Bill – My feelings for him are so deep I could weep with joy. Oh Father thank you, thank you, thank you for him. We prayed again over the phone tonight. God, he is a man who loves you so much and that makes me love him even more. Father I lift up our relationship to you. Please bless it, keep it pleasing to you. Use us together for you.

As I got to know Shalita better, I found her background and Indian heritage fascinating. She talked about growing up on the campus of the Institute in Allahabad, about the mischief she and Chutku would get into, and about the close-knit Christian community that had developed in a region of the world dominated by other faiths. My knowledge of India and its long history was limited, but she appreciated that I was genuinely interested in her background and culture—something that was apparently lacking in her marriage.

During the time that we dated, Shalita's house was about a twenty-minute drive from my home. Sometimes we would meet at a casual restaurant called Brookfields near I-80 at Madison Avenue, halfway between our two homes. One evening, after meeting there for dinner, we were leaving the restaurant in our respective cars when a song came over the radio—"In This Life" by Collin Raye. The song struck something deep inside me. I had told Shalita about this song, and when it came on we were both stopped at a red light. I jumped out of my car and ran back to her car to tell her to turn on the radio. She did and we smiled and kissed.

"I love you," I blurted out.

At that moment my entire body felt saturated with love for Shalita. In my blissful state my heart was forever bound to hers. It was intoxicating.

**

As our relationship grew we both tried hard to support one another. It was hugely important to me that Shalita believed in me and she showed it in so many ways. Whether it was a small note that she would write me and quietly slip in my luggage when I traveled for work, or when I would ramble on about some crazy idea I had for a business, she listened and supported me. She never showed anything but confidence in my abilities and potential and her support meant a great deal to me. Similarly, she valued the support and encouragement she felt from me.

We had so much fun when we were dating (what she would call *our courtship*). In time it was something we came to cherish, a special time in our lives when we got to know each other better and grew ever closer. We got along amazingly well and rarely argued. As our relationship matured, I also saw emerge a rather determined and sometimes stubborn side of Shalita that I hadn't seen before. One of these instances in particular highlighted our personality differences. We would later think back and laugh about the story, although it wasn't funny at the time and nearly derailed our relationship.

Shalita, Dryw, and I were in Southern California visiting her parents. It was July 1993. The three of us, along with Shalita's mom and my niece Sara, went to Disneyland. Dryw was only six at the time and, like most kids, was very excited to be there and bounced from one ride to another, from one store to another. At the end of the day we were all tired. It was about ten o'clock when we left. Our first stop was to drop my niece off at her grandparents' house in Whittier. I found myself in an unfamiliar area and the road was dark. Before I knew it, I saw something in the road just ahead of me. I hit my brakes, but it was too late. I felt the car rise and then come down with a crash. I cringed, not knowing what I had hit and certain my Oldsmobile was damaged. I pulled to the side of the road. As I got out I looked under the Olds, expecting to see the worst. Fortunately, nothing was obviously broken or damaged.

I looked back to see that I had run over a car's wheel in the middle of the street. I walked back and moved it to the side, not wanting others to encounter the same fate. About fifty yards ahead of us was an old, tired-looking Ford Maverick, with, you guessed it, three wheels. I was angry. I knew that wheels only fall off when a car has been severely neglected or abused, and someone's negligence would probably cost me dearly at the shop.

Although thankful my car was drivable, I was still uncertain if my car had sustained damage. I was miffed. *Why did these people leave the wheel in the middle of the road?* I wondered to myself. As I got back in the car and pulled back out on to the road, mumbling under my breath at these morons, Shalita said, "Shouldn't we go back and see if those people are ok?" *See if they are ok? These people nearly destroyed my car! They got what they deserved,* I thought to myself.

I turned to Shalita, trying my best to disguise my annoyance at this clearly ridiculous question. "They looked fine to me and it's not a bad neighborhood, so I don't think we should go back." But this response was unacceptable to her and she pushed back: "I think we need to go back and help them." We went back and forth. I didn't help that my future mother-in-law was in the car and she was surely making mental notes as the exchange continued. After we were a good two miles from the incident, Shalita said: "I insist that we go back." *Insist?* I could see the stakes were clearly very high now, and to argue further at this point would be a damaging blow to our relationship.

Steaming, I reluctantly turned the car around to see if these irresponsible people were "ok." Everyone in the car was silent as we made our way back to the scene. I was pleased to see that both the car and people were gone. "Looks like they're fine," I said, smirking. I turned the car around and we finally continued on our way.

We had many discussions afterward about the incident, each of us certain that our own perspective was right. Our informal polling of friends and family later showed that most of the women backed Shalita's view, but, perhaps not surprisingly, most men sided with me. After all, I was driving with two women, one teenage girl, and a little boy, and it might not have been safe to stop. It took some time for each of us to let go of our pride and see the others' point of view. I saw in Shalita someone more determined than I had realized, and she saw a side of me that was, at least during this incident, less than compassionate. While I felt a certain sense of confidence and conviction in my behavior that summer night, my view has changed over years. What is clear today is that I was focused on the negligence that had resulted in potential damage to my car. Shalita, however, was trying to do the right thing and was simply being the Good Samaritan.

***

The Proposal

During the summer of 1993, we both were trying to figure out if this was going to be a short-term relationship or one that would lead to marriage—what we both ultimately wanted. By August, the bumps and bruises we had sustained that summer seemed to disappear between us and we grew closer than ever. One evening, in early October, we went to see the movie *The Fugitive* with Harrison Ford. While exciting, the movie certainly was not romantic, but oddly enough, an overwhelming feeling hit me.

Like a wave washing over me, and seemingly out of the blue, I knew then and there that I wanted to marry Shalita. I put my arm around her and gave her a little squeeze. "Remember this moment," I said. She smiled, looked at me a bit puzzled, wondering what was going on in my head. Months later I told her that the little squeeze I gave her was the exact moment in time that I knew, with certainty, I wanted to spend the rest of my life with her.

I soon began to think of how and when to propose to her. I wanted to surprise her. In November, my sister, Lori, and I went shopping for a ring, looking at dozens and learning about the all-important "four Cs." Eventually, I decided on a ring at Ben Bridge jewelers in downtown Sacramento and began to plan for the big day.

In late November, I asked Shalita if we could spend the day together on Saturday, December 11, 1993. I was a bit vague about what we would do that day, but she readily agreed. To keep her from getting any hints of what I was up to, I told her a few days before the trip that I thought I was coming down with a cold and we might have to cancel—a clever fib. The plan was that she was to come to my condo early in the morning (it was no small feat to convince her it would be worth getting up so early) and we would spend the day together.

Rather than telling her where we were going that special day, I simply said we were heading toward the coast. When the morning arrived, she pulled in a bit late, smiling but grumbling about the ungodly hour. The December sky looked threatening, with dark clouds, and a cold wind was beginning to blow. The surprise plan was to fly south to spend the day in San Diego, propose after a picnic lunch, and fly back to Sacramento that evening. I schemed for weeks to plan the details. Here is how she chronicled the events of that special day.

December 28, 1993

Today Mom and I chose a wedding dress together. It's like a dream . . . Thank you Lord. Everyone around us is so happy and God is getting all the glory. I never did write down in detail how Bill proposed to me – so, for all posterity here is the story.

A week earlier he asked me at Mark Janzen's (wild) birthday party at Woody's if he could take me out to dinner on Dec. 11. He said we could go out of town, perhaps to the coast for the day and then dinner. And to bring a nice change of clothes. He also said to be at his place at 6:30 am Saturday. I groaned – 6:30! And told Bill it had better be worth it! Meanwhile, the next week was so stressful at work, I was tired. I didn't see Bill all week because he was out every evening.

He also told me that he wasn't feeling too good and not to expect too much from the weekend. Saw Bill Friday night at John's play and Lori, John, Bill and I had coffee at a coffee shop after the play. The next morning John's alarm went off at 5 am [Shalita had stayed with him that night] instead of 6 am! It was funny because it was all dark and I was so tired but dressed and then realized the time!! Got to Bill's place at 6:40 am and he drove. We got on I-5 heading north – "where are we going?" I asked. He smiled, "I thought we would go to Zamora (an old joke)." Then he said we'd go to Redding. Before I knew it he took the exit to the airport! "Where are we going?" "To the airport," he said. "Why," I responded. "We're going to San Diego for the Day!" I was absolutely dumbfounded! No!!

I was so excited! What a great surprise – what an adventure. I couldn't stop smiling. The storm hit as we left Sacramento. Got into San Diego. So beautiful! Went to Alamo car rental where a lovely white Cadillac was waiting for us. I was <u>so</u> excited. Went to Seaport Village. Walked around – went to Mistletoe, a quaint Christmas shop and bought an ornament with our names on it for our first Christmas. I was hungry and had twisted my ankle. My sweetheart made me sit down and went in search of a muffin for me. My heart swelled with love at his tenderness.

Then we drove to Horton's Plaza. Everything there was so beautiful. Looked at the shops. Then I saw a Jessica McClintock store and tried to be subtle about looking at some wedding gowns with Bill right there! Went to Farmer's

Market – a fabulous deli – and got a scrumptious picnic lunch and wine. I kept packing paper napkins, plastic forks, etc. and he said, "don't worry, it's all taken care of." Then we drove to Point Loma in Cabrillo National Park. It was breathtaking – seagulls, waves crashing – so beautiful. Bill spread out our food and from his bag he pulled out the black and white checkered napkins (like our trip to Coloma!!), wine glasses, silverware – the works. He even had biscotti for me, which he picked up from the coffee shop the night before. We had a wonderful picnic.

It was getting cold. We took pictures and then walked over to the visitor's center and looked around. We came outside and walked around. Bill was so precious – my ankle was hurting and he carried me for a bit! "Let's go on this trail here," he said. We walked on a deserted nature trail and then he found a place for us to sit. We sat overlooking the ocean. It was gorgeous! "I have something for you," he said. He pulled a letter out of his pocket and handed it to me. As I read it and came across the part where he asked me to marry him, I looked over at my sweetheart and he had a box open with a gorgeous ring *"will you marry me?"* he asked me, tears streaming down his face. I'll never forget the love and tenderness on his face. I couldn't speak. "Will you babe?" "Yes," I said and we hugged, fell back laughed and I cried and laughed and cried again. It was like time stood still and there was no one else in the world but us. I was so excited and screamed!! As we walked back to the car we passed an older couple and I said, "This wonderful man just asked me to marry him!" "Oh, that's nice," they said. It was so funny! It began to rain and as we got back in the car the storm broke. But it was sunshine and rainbows in the car.

We prayed together. It took a while for it to hit me – I was stunned and every time it hit me there was this incredible surge of joy and peace. We then drove to a book and music store. I was floating and so was Bill. We went to La Jolla for dinner – fabulous posh restaurant – La Valencia's Sky Room (waiters in tuxedos!). Bill didn't have a dinner jacket, which was required, so they let him wear one about 4 sizes too big. It was so funny. Had a wonderful candlelit dinner, champagne – very elegant. Drove back to the rental car place and then to the airport. My fiancé bought me a red rose at the airport! The flight back had only 2 other passengers on board! So funny. The stewardess announced our engagement on board and the other 2 passengers applauded!! Called Mom and Dad and Dryw from the airport. Everyone was thrilled. Jesus praise you. This day was PERFECT. Please let our wedding day be as perfect. I come back to this memory and smile. I am so blessed. My Bill – I love him so.

Chapter 4

A Life Together

The next several months were very busy as we prepared for the wedding, set for June 18, 1994. It was a time that was both exciting and exhausting. The day before the wedding was the rehearsal at the church, followed by dinner for the wedding party. The dinner was a casual meal in the backyard of my parents' house, and the talk of the day was OJ Simpson being chased in the infamous white Bronco by the Los Angeles police.

That evening I went home to my condo for the last time. With the wedding the next morning and all the changes that lay in store, I knew it would be difficult to sleep. Despite taking a sleeping pill, I still couldn't get to sleep.

We asked our pastor Cal Stevens to officiate, and a longtime family friend and pastor, Harvey Harper, to participate in the ceremony. Harvey's wife, Dorothy, had been my mom's best friend since the eighth grade. Harvey had also married my parents in 1955 and many years later had married my sister Susan. Dorothy had been my kindergarten teacher as well, so it was both comforting and a privilege to ask Harvey to assist in our ceremony.

As the ceremony began, Cal went over last-minute details with me in a side room at the church. I felt tremendous excitement, but also nervous. When the time came, the pastors, my groomsmen, and I walked out in front of the sanctuary. What I remember most clearly during those moments is the overwhelming feeling of joy and humbleness at seeing little Dryw, then seven, walking straight and tall down the aisle. He was our proud and handsome ring bearer. Despite wearing dress shoes that didn't fit well and that were hurting his feet, he beamed.

Next came Shalita, escorted down the aisle by her father, looking calm and proud. An even stronger sensation washed over me and I had to focus my attention to keep my emotions in check. Here we are, I thought, experiencing the full blossoming of our many months of courtship and engagement.

Shalita was a stunning bride. As she slowly walked down the aisle, she looked so full of joy, with an air of peaceful calm and a sweet smile on her face. I remember thinking, *this is really happening—we're really getting married!*

One of the special parts of the wedding was when we presented Dryw with a special medallion. Shalita had heard from a friend about the idea of a family medallion, and we both agreed that it would be the perfect way to honor Dryw as the three of us became a new family together. I explained the significance of the family medallion and bent down to place it around his neck. Excited, he looked like he was going to pop.

As we shared our vows, the reality of all that lay ahead for us as a married couple became more real. The wedding was both beautiful and meaningful as we tried to make it an expression of not just our love for each other, but also a way to recognize Dryw, and, above all, to acknowledge God and his blessings from which this marriage was formed. We also wanted the ceremony to reflect our steadfast commitment before family and friends for a long and loving marriage, one strong enough to withstand the rocky roads and storms that we would inevitably endure.

After the wedding ceremony, we gathered in a tightly packed hall a few miles away to continue the celebration. We were utterly exhausted when we finally left the reception. As our life began together as husband and wife, cans tied to the bumper of my car, we headed west towards the tiny, picturesque village of Sausalito on the San Francisco Bay.

Because of a mix up at the inn where we had planned to stay the first two nights, we were offered a houseboat in the Sausalito marina. But our excitement quickly faded when we learned that the accommodations for our first night of marriage was a tired, musty smelling houseboat. The mattress was very soft and I knew instantly that my back would not do well in that bed. What was going to be special, our first night together, was turning into a major disappointment. Tired and deflated, I drew a heavy sigh. Seeing my frustration, Shalita got on the phone and found a Hilton in South San Francisco, next to the airport. We quickly drove to it, and while it was hardly what we both had imagined for the first night of our honeymoon, the room was quiet, the mattress nice and firm. We collapsed.

Despite getting a good night's rest, I felt like I had a hangover the next morning, the result of weeks of preparations for the wedding and a deficit of adequate sleep. After a leisurely morning we stopped in nearby Berkeley. Shalita wanted to take me to Pasand, a south Indian restaurant not far from the UC Berkeley campus. That was my first experience with dosas, a huge, thin, crepe-like dish rolled up a little bit like a burrito, stuffed with spiced vegetables and potatoes and accompanied by a traditional spicy brown sauce. It is a staple in the Madras region. I fell in love with dosas.

Our plans for our second night were to stay at the inn I had originally booked in Sausalito. The disappointing experience with the houseboat tainted our view, so we cancelled and decided to stay in Sacramento at my condo instead. It was fun staying there because no one knew we were in town, and it gave us a chance to catch our breath after all the excitement surrounding the wedding.

On day three we headed north on I-5 toward our destination of Victoria, British Columbia. We made frequent stops along the way, enjoying the beautiful wildflowers at the base of Mount Shasta and the lush, green coniferous forests in western Oregon. Since Victoria is on Vancouver Island, we took my car by ferry from Port Angeles, Washington, which allowed us to do some exploring on the massive island.

Victoria was just as I remembered it—hanging flower baskets adding color along the clean, orderly streets. Plenty of quaint restaurants and souvenir shops added to the city's charm, and we enjoyed pleasant temperatures and lots of blue sky. It was during our visit to Victoria that I discovered Shalita's true affinity for tea. Before we were married I knew that she enjoyed tea, but when we went to the historic Empress Hotel—an elegant and enormously popular destination—she learned they served afternoon tea and she was absolutely thrilled. Tea at the Empress, while pricey, was quite an affair. Reservations had to be made and they enforced a strict dress code (I actually had to wear a jacket). Like her coffee, Shalita never took tea plain, as I did, but rather in the British tradition with milk and sugar—*lots* of milk and sugar. (I used to tease her: "Would you like some tea with your milk and sugar?"). Tea at the Empress is a time-honored tradition, with all the pomp and elegance of Victorian England. Along with tea, our ever-doting server brought us scones and crumpets. Shalita loved it all.

After several days of shopping and sightseeing in central Victoria, we visited the beautiful Butchart Gardens. For the next leg of the trip we drove several hours northwest to the tiny community of Tofino. The drive gave us a glimpse of the island outside of more touristy Victoria. After dining on fresh crab and walking along the rugged coastline, we left Tofino and headed back to our bed and breakfast in Victoria for a few more days before heading home.

We spent our last evening in Victoria driving around the city, admiring the beautiful homes, and saying our farewell to this charming town, which we enjoyed like a new friend. Not long after the sun had set, we parked the car near a small harbor and looked east towards Washington. Sitting quietly in my Oldsmobile, we watched the sky grow darker. Stars danced on the water like small angels ahead of us. The voice of Elton John crackled on the radio, "*Can you feel the love tonight?*"

It's an image and a feeling that is deeply etched in my memory. Our minds bounced back and forth between the joy we had found on our honeymoon and the call to go home. We felt uncertain of exactly what lay ahead and wished we could stretch our trip out a bit longer. When I hear that song today, my mind goes back to that sweet moment on that June evening on Victoria's harbor.

July 11, 1994
Back home again after such a perfect honeymoon. The days fly by and it's been so long since I've stopped to reflect and write my thoughts.

Being married to Bill has brought my life to a complete circle. It fits and I feel so complete and secure. He loves me in a way Mark never did or was incapable of loving. Before the wedding I looked back on my life and reflected on the painful, as well as the good times. I love Bill in a way I never loved Mark – it's strong deep and abiding. I did love Mark when I married him (Dryw keeps asking me if I did) and I believe that I did very much, but perhaps it was a childlike love – simple, trusting and pure. It was the kind of love that could have grown and matured with time. However, I do remember feeling insecure and clingy. Not feeling good about myself and even afraid of his restlessness – I was never enough!

I love Bill with the love of a woman. It's deep, mature and solid like the love I have for my family. He brings out the best in me and I feel so loved by him that I can truly risk being my truest self. God, you have given me an incredible gift! I have never been so happy in my life. It's like you've taken all the pain, heartache and tears of the past and woven them to make a beautiful picture. I feel I have such a testimony of your faithfulness to share with the world. You do make all things beautiful in your time – you do honor the desires of our heart. You are so incredibly faithful. I love my husband with all my heart... We are tender, passionate, gentle and playful together. He is my soulmate. Bill, I love you. You are the best thing that ever happened to me. I feel so close to him. He is a wonderful dad to Dryw. How blessed I am!

***

As we settled into our new life together, we experienced many changes. It was a wonderful time, but not without its challenges. The changes were especially significant for me. I moved from my tiny condo in Sacramento, where I had lived alone for six years, to Shalita's modest house in Rocklin. In addition to moving to a different community (and now having a commute to work), I needed to get rid of a lot of my belongings just to be able to fit them into the house. But the biggest change was becoming a parent—an *instant* parent. The three of us were now a "blended family."

I knew parenting would be challenging and step-parenting even more so. Growing up in a home that had its share of dysfunction left me with a less-than-ideal set of tools to parent Dryw. As challenging as it was for me at times with Dryw, a strong-willed child diagnosed with ADHD, it was hard for him as well. Dryw was seven when we got married, and while he was very excited about having a dad to live with, my tendencies toward being the disciplinarian, and often more rigid than Shalita, were at times very difficult for him. And for Shalita, there were unique challenges as well. She had told me that she felt as a single parent that she always had to defend and protect Dryw, and it was hard for her to sometimes let go of the reins of parenting him. While Shalita had custody of Dryw, the arrangement was that he would go to his dad's house every other weekend. It was nice for Shalita and I to have some time alone, but we missed Dryw when he left, and it was often an adjustment for him to come back home after being away for the weekend.

As much as we both loved our families, they too became a source of tension. Feelings got hurt and we both struggled to learn to navigate the very different family dynamics that emerged from our new respective in-laws. In particular, Shalita felt that as much as she tried to reach out and connect with my family, there were elements of unhealthy patterns that ran deep, making it a difficult and slow process.

Some of the differences were cultural as well. One day my mom called and said they had been at Walmart in Rocklin, just a mile from our house. My parents lived about thirty minutes away, in Rancho Cordova, and Mom said they thought about stopping by to say hello but they hadn't called first and didn't want to drop in on us unannounced. When I mentioned this to Shalita she was hurt that they were in the neighborhood and didn't stop and visit. I tried to explain that they were just trying to be respectful. But this made little sense to her and she was clearly bothered by it.

Shalita's parents also lived in town, about thirty-five minutes away. Unlike my folks, the Chitambars would come over and stay the night or sometimes the weekend. Shalita loved it, but for me, it took some getting used to. The house seemed a little crowded and I had a hard time understanding why they didn't just drive home in the evening (and sleep in their beds!). Some of the discomfort we each felt came from the very different cultures we grew up in. But some of the difference was related to our families' size and dynamics. Shalita's parents both came from very large families and it was completely normal to have aunts and uncles, cousins and grandparents visiting— often staying for several days.

In contrast, my mom was an only child and my dad had a half-brother and half-sister that he barely knew. Naturally, we didn't have a lot of family dropping by the Blackburn house. Like many things that we clashed over, it wasn't a matter of right and wrong, but just

52

working through the discomfort we often felt related to growing up in very different homes and communities.

August 10, 1995

It is good to come into your presence this morning, Lord. It is so good to find you here waiting for me – smiling at me and loving me. I praise you for being my shepherd and guide – my rock and my hiding place. I adore you and praise you with my whole heart, Father, Son and Holy Spirit. You are so real – so powerful and so loving. I love you Lord and I praise you for your love and fullness.

I meditate on the passage I read today in Acts, about Lydia, the jailer and then in Kings about Elijah and the woman who ministered to him. Such fine examples of Christian hospitality. I see that all three people first believed and then opened their homes to others in your name. Oh God, when I bought this house in July 1990, I gave it to you and asked that you would help it be open and a haven for others and I ask the same even more now that it's not just Dryw and my home, but Bill's too – and the three of us as family. Enlarge the walls of our hearts and this home to be filled with love and compassion. That everyone who walks in here may feel your loving hand. That it may be a beautiful Christian home with you at the center. Father I know you have given me a key role as wife and mother, of setting the tone and heart of this home. Help me to be organized and efficient as I minister to my family – keep my attitude cheerful and my heart fixed on you. Please keep my priorities straight – that I may be hospitable and faithful. Give Bill that same spirit too Lord that together we may be a mighty witness for you.

Help Dryw see our home as a haven of love and peace too. Father I pray that you will continually cement my marriage and build it each day on your foundation. Please forgive me for last night and for my anger and not dealing well with it and not being sensitive to Bill.

I have so much to learn about dealing with conflict without getting upset. I need you so much to teach me. Please help me to listen better and to be more supportive and understanding, especially toward Bill.

Help us both to truly listen and understand where the other person is coming from. God I pray for Dryw that he may be strong in you. Channel his strong-willed nature into a positive stream and show us how to do that. Help me to be more patient and consistent and to listen to what he says. Please give Bill and I wisdom as we raise him. Please protect him from evil influences. Bless this coming school year for him – his teacher and classmates, and may it be a good year for him.

September 1, 1995
Happy new month. Father I come to you this morning feeling so weak and more than ever I need your cleansing and filling. I feel sad inside and I don't know how much of it is hormonal, fatigue or what. But I know God that you are faithful and true and that you love me and so I come to your presence truly needing your touch. Please fill me Lord – give me peace, strengthen me and give me lightness of spirit.

I feel overwhelmed on every side. I am feeling frustrated, angry and sad and I rest in you. Please cleanse me. I feel hurt – please take that away. Lift me out of this depression and set my feet on your rock. Lord increase my faith. God I pray for my marriage. It is good and I love Bill so much. I am having such a hard time with conflict and it drains me. I have felt anger toward him and certain situations and struggle with feelings of inadequacy within myself in terms of whether I'm a good wife. I feel at times I am but other times I feel so inadequate. I know there is much going on with Bill and I wish he would talk more with me . . . I feel we've taken such a beating this past year . . . I hear myself and I sound childish but God I feel broken and sad and somehow cheated. Please give me your perspective. You know my deepest desires and prayers. I give them to you. I love you Lord. Thank you for

loving me in my brokenness and meeting me right where I am.
I give myself to you.

Amen

Chapter 5

A Trip Home

A few months after we got married, we began to discuss the possibility of taking a trip to India. The more we discussed it, the more excited both of us became about the idea. In the spring of 1995 we began to plan our trip in earnest, and decided the best time to go would be during the upcoming winter break.

We planned to leave in late December, but as mid-November came around, I remember feeling anxious. We only had six weeks until our departure to India, and I felt unprepared for this major journey. The excitement we had felt talking and planning for the trip turned into one mixed with a good deal of apprehension. We still had shots to get, visas to apply for, reservations to complete, and a lot of packing to do.

Panic began to creep in. Myriad thoughts raced through my head. *What if we get sick? What if we become separated in one of those crowed Delhi train stations? Can we really afford this trip?* So much uncertainty lay ahead. Although it was my idea for the three of us to go on this trip, I couldn't help thinking that maybe this wasn't such a good idea. But the airline tickets had already been purchased and we were all excited about going.

The trip was important to each of us. For Shalita, it would be the first time since leaving India that she would see her friends, aunts and uncles, cousins, her home. For Dryw, it meant visiting this far-away land he was connected to (when he was seven he would tell people that he was "half India and half America"). For me, I was excited about meeting Shalita's relatives and childhood friends and experiencing a part of the world I knew little about.

On December 27, 1995, we started our journey, leaving the comfort and security of our home and heading for what to me seemed a strange and exotic land. The first leg of the trip included an uneventful, but utterly exhausting twenty-hour flight to Singapore, which included a short layover in Seoul, Korea. After a restless night in Singapore, we boarded another Boeing 747 for a six-hour flight to the Indira Gandhi International Airport in the nation's capital, New Delhi.

I remember looking down at the ground from a few thousand feet in the air and seeing the lights of Delhi. *We made it!* I was perhaps more tired than excited at that point and just wanted to get off the plane, make it through customs with minimal hassle, find our hotel, and sleep!

It was not that simple. As we began our descent, I noticed a strange smoky smell on the plane. *Where was the smoke coming from?* I thought. Then it dawned on me that this sulfur-laden smell was coming from the Delhi air, which was slowly seeping into our plane. If the air quality was this bad a few thousand feet up, I thought it must be really bad on the ground. I was stunned. When we got off the plane I realized that I could not only smell the smoke inside the airport, but could see a haze hanging over the flood of passengers streaming in and out of the complex of adjoining buildings.

About 9:30 p.m. local time we made our way through customs and converted some of our dollars to rupees. We hired a taxi to take us to our hotel in suburban New Delhi. As we approached our tired-looking black Hindustan Ambassador, the ubiquitous Indian taxicab, seemingly unchanged for decades, the smell of diesel exhaust from dozens of idling taxis, mixed with local smoke, made the air nearly unbreathable. We climbed in the back seats, slammed the door shut, and pulled away from the airport.

Looking ahead I saw hanging beads, images of Krishna or Shiva—or perhaps other Hindu gods dangling from the rearview mirror. Our driver was a short, dark man who spoke no English. Although Shalita's first language was English, she had been taught Hindi in school. Despite her worries that she was rusty, her ability to converse with the driver in Hindi came back immediately.

One of the first things I noticed as we pulled away from the curb was that there were no seatbelts. *This is not good*, I thought. It wasn't long before it became apparent to me that driving in India was vastly different from anything I had experienced. The street was teeming with activity. Motorized rickshaws, bicycles, and occasional men walking with a water buffalo spilled into the street. As we raced down the road through the hazy dark, our driver weaved in and out of traffic, either honking or flashing his lights to warn drivers and pedestrians to "watch out." Of course driving on the left side of the road didn't help calm my nerves, and I realized that nowhere on earth are seatbelts more needed!

After what could best be described as a "white knuckles" ride, we were close to our destination, but could not find the hotel. All of us strained to look out of the dirty windows for the Bright Star Inn, our home for the next few nights. Frustration grew as midnight approached and no one along the street could give us directions to the hotel. Finally we called out to a man who was getting out of his car. We were relieved that he said he knew how to get to our hotel and suggested that we follow his car. The stranger was a tall man with a large stomach. He spoke perfect English. He told us that the taxi drivers often rip off tourists and then turned to our driver and proceeded to chide him in Hindi. He ended his scolding with a slap to our taxi driver's face. Through my foggy mental state I remember thinking, *did he just hit our driver? He did!* While we were not happy that the driver hadn't found the hotel, we were shocked at the stranger's aggression. The most important thing, we told ourselves, was getting safely to the hotel.

We followed the stranger around a few corners and became concerned when he made a U-turn. Did he really know where he was going? Then our driver stopped following the stranger who was guiding us and proceeded in a different direction. Things did not look good. Shalita argued with our driver to follow the stranger, who seemed to be our best hope. We continued down the road and eventually reunited with the stranger. We followed his car and finally reached our destination, weary, but relieved we had arrived at the hotel.

As the stranger quickly approached our car, he explained why he made a U-turn and flew into Hindi, again chewing out our driver. Along with a scolding louder than the first, came another slap to the face. *Unbelievable.* Needless to say, it had not been a good night for us—or our driver. We paid our driver what we had negotiated to get to our destination and added a generous tip for his trouble. He was clearly unhappy and demanded more money. While we were sympathetic, we had been warned not to overpay taxis and to not go above the negotiated price. He finally left, no doubt wishing he had picked up an easier ride.

We crawled up the stairs to the Bright Star Inn, found our room, and got Dryw to bed. The room was a bit rundown, a disappointing end to a long and exhausting day. Shalita was discouraged and felt badly about my introduction to India. "This is not what I wanted for our first night here," she said, tears streaming down her cheeks. I told her it would be fine and held her close. It was 2:30 a.m. when we finally collapsed into bed.

***

Fortunately, the rest of our journey was much better than that first long evening. The next day we visited with some friends, including Shalita's childhood friend, Chutku. We met Chutku at her sister Dipti's apartment. Chutku, Dipti, and the rest of the family grew up next to the Chitambars and their father also worked at the Allahabad Agricultural Institute.

Dipti's apartment was on the second floor. I noticed a noise from outside and wandered over to the balcony. "Street vendors," Dipti said. "Go out and see them." This was one of my first views into a yet unknown world. Men and women were selling fresh produce from the back of large bicycles. One man was hollering out something, and I soon learned he was collecting scrap metal in the neighborhood. Another man had a bicycle completely laden with various toys and balloons for sale. The most intriguing vendor, however, was the monkey man.

The bald, middle-aged man carried two monkeys with him to entertain kids. He wore a week's worth of gray stubble on his broad face. As he squatted to the ground and prepared for the show, I noticed his shoes had no laces. The two monkeys wore collars; one had a dark red scarf, the other a tiny, dusty, green dress. With his stick, the man prodded them to perform. They jumped through rings, pulled a miniature wooden cart and carried out other acrobatics. The monkeys dutifully performed their tricks to the rhythm of a small hand drum. It was both fascinating and distressing. Here was a poor man with two animals that had the look of weary, abused carnival animals—small, poor creatures whose spirits had long since been broken. It was a curiosity, one of many we encountered on our trip.

We stayed with another family friend that evening named Margaret, who had a flat in a very nice part of New Delhi. "Aunty

Margaret," as we called her, had gone to school with Shalita's parents when they were attending Cornell in the 1950s. Well educated (and with strong opinions), she took good care of us for the next few days and helped us plan the next leg of our trip. Shalita explained to Dryw that he was to call her "Aunty," a colloquial term of endearment in India for children to call family friends. As a result, Dryw found he had many uncles and aunties during the visit.

The first leg of our trip in and around New Delhi was spent with friends, which Shalita relished, and it allowed Dryw and me to acclimate to our new surroundings. We then left the congestion and smoke of New Delhi, heading south to the state of Rajasthan and to Jaipur, the historic Pink City. To get there, we hired a taxi and rode along a crowded and sometimes dangerous highway. There we found traffic as bad as or worse than what we had experienced in Delhi, but with less smoke and haze.

Jaipur's colorful stone structures were impressive. We hired a cheerful guide who showed us the Ambar Palace and City Palace, both hundreds of years old, and told us stories of a past dominated by powerful and wealthy Rajas. There we visited a rug factory while in Jaipur and watched artisans weaving rugs, much as they have done for centuries. We bought a beautiful, small, burgundy silk rug as a memento of our trip.

After leaving Jaipur, we headed east for the next leg of our trip. After we had been on the road a few hours, I suggested to our taxi driver that we pull over so that we could take a quick break and stretch our legs. We stopped at a wide spot in the road, in the shade of a large tree. Anxious to stretch my tired back, I jumped out first, followed by Shalita and Dryw. The noise of branches shaking in the tree above startled us. Instinctively, we all looked up. Just then a monkey fell from the tree to the ground, just a few feet from where Shalita and Dryw were standing. They dashed back to the taxi, jumped in and slammed the door shut. The monkey, as frightened as it was, ran for the tree and, in a flash, climbed back up the trunk. As I looked up, I could see there were probably twenty monkeys in the tree and I laughed out loud at the scene.

Continuing east, we made our way to Agra and India's most famous treasure, the Taj Mahal. After another tiring drive, we reached the city at night, anxious to see this majestic, ivory-colored marble giant. From 1631 to 1653, it took more than twenty thousand workers to complete this mausoleum, which the ruler Shah Jahan built for Mumtaz Mahal, his third and favorite wife.

We were surprised and a bit disappointed the next morning to find the Taj Mahal shrouded in a thick fog. As we toured the grounds, the fog slowly lifted, giving us a chance to capture its magnificence on film. Gradually the image became stronger. Then it faded faster than it had appeared, as the fog returned like arms wrapping around this giant. We left grateful that we were able to get a glimpse of this stunning historic site.

Next we traveled to Allahabad, Shalita's birthplace. Like much of India, it had changed a great deal since she left in the early 1980s. Arriving at the Agricultural Institute transported Shalita back to her childhood. This small Christian college just off the banks of the Yamuna River was where Shalita's father had taught and had later become its president. It was on this small campus that Shalita had grown up, an isolated and somewhat sheltered world but filled with the cultural and academic riches of campus life.

As we walked around the campus, we met up with Shalita's family cook, Sarju. It was an emotional reunion. They hugged and cried. After catching up, Sarju's wife brought out beautiful handmade baskets and trivets made of colored straw. We bought several for friends and ourselves. Over the next few days, Shalita introduced Dryw and me to a number of former neighbors, with whom we had several teas and Christmas cakes (what we would call fruitcake). While meeting old friends and seeing the Institute was quite interesting for Dryw and me, it was bittersweet for Shalita. It was hard for her to see how the Institute had declined under inconsistent leadership.

We also ventured out into the city for some sightseeing. Allahabad is a holy city to Hindus. It is a place where two great rivers, the Ganges and the Yamuna, come together. This confluence, or "sangam" brings thousands of Hindus to bathe in the waters in search of spiritual cleansing. When we went to the edge of the river, we were able to witness a fascinating annual gathering called Magh mela, which drew Indians from around the region.

At the shore of the river, we could see people hiring boats that would row well out into the river. The boats were long, probably twenty-five feet or more in length. Each boat had one rower and up to two dozen occupants. When we inquired about hiring one, we determined that the rates were reasonable, so we decided to have our own boat—no need to be in a crowded boat when we could have one to ourselves.

We carefully climbed into the boat and settled in. We quickly shoved off. Our captain said very little but competently rowed us out into the middle of the river where there was a large wooden platform tethered to the riverbed. As our boat pulled up alongside this dock in the middle of this vast river, we noticed people bathing. This was strictly ceremonial. Two men in long beards appeared and began talking with Shalita in Hindi. I had little idea what they were talking about until she stopped and told me. "He wants us to buy some coconut and marigolds," she said. I reached into my pocket and pulled out some rupees, which she handed to the man. He gave her this dried concoction and seemed to be instructing her what to do next.

Before I knew it, the discussion had become heated and as I looked around, I noticed that our boat's captain had disappeared. Here the three of us were in a boat quite a distance from the safety of the shore, Shalita was arguing with the men about I didn't know what, and our captain was nowhere in sight. Not understanding a word of Hindi, I was concerned that we might be offending these men. About this time, Shalita threw the marigolds into the river and the men wandered off. When I asked her what was going on she said that one of the men wanted her to say a prayer and she refused, telling him that we were Christians—hence the commotion. Our captain then reappeared, climbed back into the boat, and we quietly headed for the shore.

Leaving Allahabad, we embarked on a four-hour train ride to Lucknow to visit Shalita's family. There we were able to meet several relatives that until then I had only heard about. I met Anita, Shalita's cousin, and her husband, John. They were about the same age as Shalita and me and I immediately felt a connection with them. Dryw and I enjoyed hearing stories about the cousins as they were growing up. It was there that I also met Shalita's Aunty Helen, her mother's sister. Aunty Helen was warm and gracious. One night she cooked for all of us and, to this day, I still remember the fragrant biryani rice she made. Filled with nuts, raisins, and a few vegetables, it was the best rice dish I have ever had.

While Lucknow had little sightseeing to offer us, the time there with her family made it the highlight of our trip. Memories linger of the distinctive scent of cardamom and curries, and the sound of laughter from childhood stories told around the small dining table.

Our final trek brought us back to New Delhi, where bargaining with the shopkeepers for clothes and souvenirs consumed our final days. Fortunately, we found the air there much clearer. As our departure day drew closer, we longed to return home, but felt sadness as well. Our trip was filled with adventure, intrigue, and emotion, memories that we would always cherish. Beyond the inconveniences that invariably accompany traveling abroad, we treasured the times talking and laughing with family and friends and left with a desire to someday return. In the novel *Life of Pi,* Yann Martel refers to the "rich, noisy and functioning madness of India"— an apt description of our experience.

I consider India one of the most important trips in my life. Not so much because it was distant and exotic, but because it brought the three of us closer together. It was Shalita's only trip back to India. She told me when we returned home not only how much the trip had meant to her, but that she appreciated that I wanted to travel there as a family and experience her heritage in a new way.

Chapter 6

An Addition to the Family

We returned home from India in late January, weary from the trip and the long flight home but eager to share our adventure with family and friends. In April we received some exciting news.

April 22, 1996
I am pregnant! Found out on Good Friday and even though we had been trying, I was still stunned when the doctor told me my test was positive. Everyone is thrilled! I am excited too despite how awful I feel with nausea and fatigue. It is a miracle happening inside me and this will be a positive and blessed pregnancy. I can't imagine a baby after so long. My bond with Dryw is so powerful and intense and I can't imagine that intensity with another child and yet I know it will be unique and powerful too. I have felt shaky emotionally and was a grump with Bill yesterday.

October 1, 1996
Almost seven months pregnant! The child within me grows each day by leaps and bounds – kicking, stretching and moving around. Such a precious miracle of God. I marvel at his handiwork as He knits the inner parts of our baby together. The past few months have been good. First trimester was tough and I'm glad I had the summer off. Now I'm in my last trimester – I feel big. Everyone says I look beautiful and I feel it too! Our baby will probably be a boy judging from the ultrasound – Daniel Benedict Owen Blackburn. Thank you Lord for a new month and a new life!

Shalita relished the idea of being a mother of two and in the excitement of us having a baby together. Unlike her pregnancy with

Dryw, which was a time of intense conflict and shattered trust, she felt doubly blessed by our stable marriage relationship. We discussed for months what name to give the baby and settled on Daniel. For middle names we chose Benedict after Shalita's father and Owen after my father. Daniel arrived in late November and we brought him home on Thanksgiving, which made for a particularly special day.

As she did for Dryw, Shalita started a special journal of letters to Daniel.

January 26, 1997

My precious beautiful son Daniel,

You are almost 2 months old and I have wanted to write you a letter since your birth day. Words seem so inadequate to express the depth of love I have in my heart for you. You are truly God's gift and blessing to your dad and me. We are awed by your beauty, purity and innocence. We marvel at what God has made through us – the wonder and miracle of your precious life moves me deeply – I love you so much...

This is the first of many letters to you from me, which I will record in this journal. When you are an adult you can read this and perhaps understand who your mom was and some of the ways she felt about you in life. This is my legacy to you.

I will never forget the day you were born. I had been in preterm labor 4 weeks before you were born and had to have complete bed rest – not fun! We had a couple of false alarms and then at 3:30 a.m. my water broke and we knew this was it! We were all so excited! Dryw was ready to be dropped off at his friend Haley's house in less than 5 minutes – a true record for him! He kept saying, "Our baby will be here!!" Dad was very calm and only ran through one red light on the way to the hospital. Nana and Mama [Shalita's parents] and Uncle John arrived at 6:30 a.m. and Ann was there too. Linda arrived at 8. The nurses were wonderful and caring. Your dad was wonderful. I kept looking into his eyes – drawing strength from him as I worked to push you out. Dad and Mama were there on either side as you emerged. I heard you cry and I cried too. What a miracle – seeing you come out of me so whole and perfectly formed.

After you were cleaned up we all prayed and Nana blessed you. Daniel Benedict Owen – child of the Kingdom – precious boy you are blessed indeed. You have been born into a family who knows and loves Jesus and where we strive to make Jesus Lord of our home and lives. You have 4 wonderful grandparents, uncles and aunts and cousins, a big brother who couldn't wait for you to get here and parents who love each other deeply and love you so much. We are committed to giving you a wonderful secure home and childhood – deep roots of faith in Jesus. I pray that I may be the best possible mother to you and that you may grow to be a man after God's own heart.

Dryw says I'm now a mother of two sons and I am thrilled by that. Just saying "my children" or "my sons" is exciting.

Daniel, you are so beautiful! You are a gorgeous color – big dark eyes, long fingers and a great combination of your dad and me! You look so much like Dryw did as a baby, it's amazing. We are completely in love with our 6 lb., 14 oz., 22½ inch package!

You started smiling last week and completely melt us!
Precious Baby Daniel you are God's gift to us!

All my love,
Mom

May 2, 1997

My little Banny,

I'm watching you lie on the bed and squeal, smile and pump your legs in the air. My heart just dissolves. At 5 months, you grow more beautiful and precious with each day. You are a delightful baby – so easy going, happy and content. I have never been so fulfilled or happy and content in my life. You rolled over last week and are just delighted with yourself. I love hearing you laugh and you laugh a lot. You have been sleeping right through the night for a couple of months now and it's great! You are also loving rice cereal and veggies.

Daniel, so many people love and cherish you. As my mom says you are the embodiment of everyone's love. Those big dark eyes and big cheeks melt all those around you. We are enjoying every minute of you.

Your baptism was on April 20 and I will never forget it. You were so perfect when Rev. Hull placed the water on you – you didn't even flinch! We are blessed in you more than I can ever say.

All my love,
Mommy

June 3, 1997

My sweet baby –

6 months old!! How time has flown. You weigh 19 lbs. 9 oz. and are 28 inches long – with your head circumference 17 ¼ inches, what a big boy! My arm muscles are really getting a workout. It is such fun watching you grow – you roll over and are trying to sit up. It's so funny to watch you sit up – you look so pleased with yourself for 30 seconds before you fall over to the side or back! These moments are so priceless. I love taking naps with you. You snuggle into the hollow of my neck and fall asleep – your breathing is the sweetest sound to me. You really love your big brother and just light up when he comes home from school. You love your daddy so much too and he is so wonderful!

Daniel – you are the joy and light of our home and our lives and you are loved more than we can ever say.

XOX Mommy

Shalita called Daniel her "sunshine boy," and he brought great joy to us both. Each evening we had rituals with Daniel before he went to bed. One was reading a favorite book to him. Another was Shalita singing to him as she tucked him in bed. Before she would say prayers with Daniel, she would sing to him a Hindi nursery rhyme:

Nini baba nini,
Makhan, Roti, Chini,
Makhan Roti Ho gaya,
Hamara baba so gaya
(Sleep my baby sleep,
Butter, bread, and sugar,
The butter and bread is gone,
My little boy fell asleep)

Like many others, this was another of Shalita's traditions that has been indelibly etched in Daniel's mind.

In many ways, the happiest times in our lives were when the boys were young. We had been married long enough to know each other well, but not so long that we didn't still feel the excitement of growing together and raising the boys. We were still young enough to enjoy good health and still had all our parents in reasonably good health. Shalita stayed home the first year with Daniel and in particular enjoyed the thrill of watching him grow from baby to little boy.

She was an outstanding mother from the experiences she had gleaned from her studies and later teaching human development, from her experiences raising Dryw as a single mom, and of course the tremendous love and security she knew from her family growing up. Shalita would say that she could see Daniel's smile begin in his eyes and would marvel at his adorable grin. We loved seeing him grow, feeling the wonderment of a healthy, happy baby developing into a unique little person. Dryw was a good big brother and it was fun watching our two boys together as they developed a special bond.

May 3, 1997 11:00 pm

In an hour I will be 38 years old. It sounds so unreal because in 2 years I will be 40 – the midpoint of my life. I feel so much growth and change within myself. This past year has truly been the best year of my life. I'm happier and more at peace than I have ever been. God is infinitely good and so faithful to me. Praise be to Him forever. In so many ways my life has come full circle. I am so fulfilled beyond measure in my family. I have a wonderful loving husband with whom I feel so secure and loved – that is one of the greatest blessings. I love Bill more and more each day. We will be married 3 years in June! Wow!!

It feels like we have always been together and indeed these past 3 years we have walked some rough paths, but with God's help we emerge stronger and deeper in love with a growing understanding of each other. Looking back on our wedding day, our love then was so new – I love us now – our love is maturing... wonderfully tender, sweet and exciting. I am so fulfilled in being a mother!! It is powerful and so intense. I love my 2 sons fiercely and protectively in such unique ways. Dryw at 10 is growing so well – a sensible and very loving boy – so perceptive and sensitive to spiritual matters. He is having such a good year. It's so neat to hear all the positive things said about him – especially what a well-mannered and fine boy he is. It is so rewarding to see all that we teach him beginning to pay off.

And then there's Daniel, my little Bobanny, who is our joy. At 5 months he is so adorable and has changed our lives and captured our hearts forever.

I am home full time with him and loving every minute. I find such joy in the simple acts of taking care of my family. God, my cup runneth over. You have taken the tears and anguish of the past and turned them around into tears of joy. You have made beauty from ashes. Thank you Jesus for my life – it is a precious gift from you. I praise you for my parents and my family.

. . . Father, as I enter this year please continue to give me your joy and peace. Make me a yielding, faithful vessel and a blessing to all around. Please give me wisdom and discretion in all my ways. Help this to be the best year ever with you at the Head and Center of my life – I love you Jesus. Amen!

***

In January 1998, Shalita started a new kind of journal. It was called *The Simple Abundance Journal of Gratitude* by Sarah Ban Breathnach. It contained a brief introduction and quotes of gratitude and thankfulness. On the blank page of the inside cover I found the tracing of two hands. The larger one said "Dryw." The smaller one, superimposed on Dryw's handprint were squiggly lines that made up Daniel's handprint. His name was barely legible and below it was written, "21 mo. 8/13/98."

On the next page, below Shalita's name, were the words from two songs: "Give thanks with a grateful heart" and part of Amy Grant's "Doubly Good to You." After the introduction was a list of one hundred and fifty "Often Overlooked Blessings." Shalita had put a star next to most of them. The list included things big and slight, small beauties and simple pleasures, including: "Answer to prayer," "not having to cook tonight," "watching the sunset." She put two stars next to: "Holding your child in your arms," "the support and loving presence of sisters and brothers," "the first kiss (April 22, 1993)," and "the precious lingering memory of your mother's sweet scent."

For the entire year, Shalita would write down things she was grateful for. It was a simple yet remarkable effort that allowed her to record the many blessings she found each day.

January 9, 1998
- Thank you Father for Bill's sensitivity in going in late for work so I could sleep in after being up all night with Daniel.
- Batches of Chicken soup made today to share with the neighbors

- A warm cozy home – especially on a damp, cold and grey day
- My dad and mum – their lives and keeping them safe
- Daniel walking into the doctor's office holding my hand.

February 17
- Coming home to the smiles and warm hugs of my sons
- Daniel's sweet smile as he ran toward me
- Bill's deep love for me expressed in a beautiful card – made me cry
- Rocking Daniel to sleep. Watching his precious face.
- Tucking Dryw in bed. Watching him grow into a fine young man.

May 11
- Waking up early and getting much done around the house
- Making delicious taco soup!
- The fulfillment I feel in taking care of my family
- Reading to Dryw after dinner
- A great day!

October 4
- Relaxing at home
- Quiet and peace in the morning over coffee and the newspaper
- Getting all my papers graded
- Daniel's sweet kisses and joys
- Visiting with Linda – how dear she is
- Dryw safely home

November
1998 is drawing to a close. One of the best things I have done this year is keeping this journal. It has helped me live each moment and as I do I am learning to live in a spirit of prayer – for prayer is gratitude to God. I am so grateful for the gift of life – breath – heartbeat. To feel, see and touch my family who I love with all my heart. I am blessed beyond measure in the security of Bill's love. Our precious sons who fulfill me and

fill us with sunshine. For our parents and their lives, as they grow older I recognize that time is a gift and time with them, each day, is a gift from God. I pray for many, many more years of good health for them.

Chapter 7

Stress Comes Knocking

When I met Shalita she had been a full-time professor at Sierra College for about three years. She was very popular on campus and had a faithful following of students and an excellent rapport with the other faculty in the Family and Consumer Sciences Department. I envied the relationship she enjoyed with her colleagues. She was especially close to the two other full-time professors in the department, Roselene Kelley and Clare Dendinger. Roselene was the veteran in the department, a warm-hearted, solid professional who was polished and a bit reserved. Clare, who had arrived at Sierra shortly after Shalita, was effervescent and quick-witted. While they each had distinctly different backgrounds and personalities, they got along very well together. They also had excellent relationships with the part-time faculty who made up the rest of the department.

In 2000, things began to change in the department. Several new faculty were hired and some pushed for a new direction for the department. While some of the ideas were welcomed and supported by the veteran faculty, others were not. Shalita became increasingly frustrated, as there seemed to be division of the "old guard" versus the new. Of course we didn't know it at the time, but it was the beginning of a series of stressors and challenges that would come our way over the course of several years. For me, it was the start of a long, difficult decade.

One of the newly hired professors began to change the culture of this close-knit group. The woman was a tall, attractive African American who had wowed Shalita and her colleagues during her interview for a faculty position at Sierra. She used a PowerPoint presentation before it was commonly used at the school and came across as a very tech savvy and polished interviewee.

I remember meeting her at our home some months after she was hired. I too was impressed with her. Before long she began to introduce new ideas at department meetings and tension began to emerge. Along with some other new faculty, the new professor felt the department was due for some updating, and she had a clear agenda to put forward. This chafed some of the senior faculty, including Shalita. From Shalita's perspective, this colleague and some of the other new hires wanted to throw out some of the very things that department faculty had worked hard to build up and nurture over the years. None were ready to "roll over" and embark on a new path. Resentments developed.

Things took a permanent turn for the worse when, on an interview panel, Shalita witnessed one of the new faculty make a gesture toward the candidate, but thinking that no one had seen it. It appeared that they were giving the candidate an advantage, something that was clearly inappropriate and unethical. Needless to say, this would be cause for discipline if this were true. While impossible to prove, Shalita stuck her neck out and brought the incident up after the interview. When she told me about the incident, I remember thinking that Shalita's accusation of professional misconduct could make her a permanent enemy of the new faculty. Without a confession or corroboration from other members of the interview panel, it would be impossible to prove, and would be Shalita's word against hers. This set the two women on a path somewhere between strong dislike and all-out loathing. Neither trusted each other after that.

The warm and collegial walls within the department that had existed for years soon began to crumble. The new professor began recruiting others in the department, especially the newest faculty members, to adopt her ideas about the department's future. One of these was a Caucasian woman who worked at another campus within the system. Shalita received a copy of a letter to the department dean by this new faculty accusing her of unprofessional conduct towards the African American professor and essentially saying she was biased because of the woman's ethnicity. Shalita was shocked. The letter caused deep hurt and Shalita, completely caught off guard, was very angry. She felt that the African American professor was using the other new professor to get back at Shalita for the accusation of misconduct during the interview. The notion that Shalita had discriminated against the woman because she was African American was, of course, ridiculous. It was almost laughable, but of course it was an accusation that the administration couldn't ignore without at least some discussion.

Feelings that had been simmering for months began to boil over. Shalita was put on the tenure committees for both women, and the mounting friction that was developing within the department was palpable. While Shalita had tremendous people skills and enjoyed a huge number of friends, it was particularly difficult for her when she didn't get along with someone. Over the course of several months I witnessed Shalita become stressed about every upcoming department or tenure committee meeting. She was clearly in the middle of a hornet's nest and things were not about to blow over anytime soon.

March 26, 2000
Blessed Lord my stronghold shield and deliverer you are truly God. How can I ever doubt your power and the fact that everything is in your hands? Lord – you know that I am in the lion's den at work – there is evil and dishonesty all around me. Yet Father, you are bigger and greater than all around me. Please be a wall of fire and protection around me. Give me boldness and wisdom to speak the truth and let that truth set all things free . . . Only you can touch hearts and change lives and I know you are already working. Let my integrity shine and be so clearly evident to all around through my speech and actions. Jesus I pray that as much as people may try to cast a shadow on me, that their lies may be truly exposed and that only what is true prevails. I love you and worship you with my whole heart. It is so good to pour out my heart to you and to know that you have known all along what is in my heart and you already know what lies ahead.

May 30, 2000
Blessed Father – this is the end of what has been so far the most difficult semester at Sierra College. I have been in the fire and am so weary and tired and yet you have so faithfully carried me and uplifted me. I praise your name that I have made it so far and that you will carry me the rest of the way. May I be like the men in the fiery furnace who emerged so clean that not even the smell of fire was in their clothes nor was their hair singed.

When the tenure committees for the two women met, they found mixed work performance. This was in part because of some bad experiences that both Shalita and some of the other faculty had with both women. After meeting for months and engaging in lengthy discussions to evaluate the two women, the final decision of both committees was to deny tenure—an outcome that was uncommon. When the decision of the two tenure committees was sent to administration, the college president made the highly unusual decision of overturning the decision of both committees. This stunning turn of events was a victory for both women, but was met with shock and disbelief by the members of the committees. Shalita, in particular, was upset. She had worked with the president at another campus years earlier in her career and the two had enjoyed a good relationship. She was certain that the president had made the decision due primarily because one of the women was African American and potentially racial overtones could emerge if the tenure denials had been upheld. Shalita felt the president was being a political animal and was therefore willing to compromise integrity to avoid a potentially ugly battle and possible bad press.

During this time, Shalita worked hard to avoid seeking retaliation. She worked hard to set aside the hurt she felt from her reputation being questioned and unfair accusation of inappropriate behavior, including racism. Being the object of intense dislike and having to be on both committees caused Shalita to walk a fine line and put her in a position she hated. While most of the staff supported Shalita and the other tenure committee members, the department was deeply and painfully divided. She felt a great deal of pressure as to how to handle the situation, but ultimately believed she had to do the right thing, which she believed in her heart she had done.

Sadly, the entire tenure episode came back to bite her. After the decisions of the tenure committees were overturned, there was an investigation into the objectivity of the committees and the appropriateness of the decision to deny tenure. Much of the focus of the investigation was Shalita's behavior. In the end, the investigation led to a report that cast doubt on Shalita's objectivity and painted her in a light that suggested she retaliated on the two women. Of course, this caused even deeper hurt for Shalita. She felt that the administration was looking for an excuse for the president to justify his overturning the committees' decisions and was using her as a scapegoat. They portrayed her as a fellow faculty member with an "axe to grind." Shalita had felt that she had given her best to Sierra College for eleven years and was now on the defensive over allegations of not being objective and inappropriately influencing the committees.

As I witnessed firsthand this ugly chapter unfolding, I could see that Shalita was mentally and physically worn down. She had experienced months of tension with a handful of faculty and now felt abandoned by the administration. She witnessed politics win over what to her were simple facts of poor performance and behind-the-scenes manipulation of the two women. I desperately wanted Shalita to leave the college, seeing the toll it was taking on her. It was bitterly ironic that what had seemed for years to be an ideal job turned into a nightmare and it was clearly eating away at her.

The ultimate slap in the face to Shalita, and to me as well, was learning that the college was going to hold a Skelly hearing for her. When she told me this, I didn't even know what a Skelly hearing was. When I searched it online, I was shocked. These unusual hearings are specifically held for public employees that are about to be disciplined. The Skelly hearing allows the employee to present their side before official disciplinary action is taken. I was furious when I learned this. What had started as serious questions about the performance and integrity of new faculty had morphed into a monster that had turned vicious, and was now about to go after Shalita. I was enraged at the injustice and the lunacy of the administration's actions. It was clear that Shalita needed to leave this toxic work environment.

As the spring 2001 semester was winding down, Shalita and I made a rather quick decision to get away. We escaped to England and France with our boys, providing a much-needed break for all of us.

May 26, 2001, American Airlines Flight 176 from LAX to Heathrow

Our dream becomes a reality. For so long we have talked and dreamed about visiting England and France and we are now finally on our way! The family trip came about very unexpectedly with Bill surfing the Internet and finding great fares to London . . . hear we are at 29,000 feet! Thank you God for this gift – for that is what this trip is – from you. After the trauma of the past year I am <u>so</u> ready for renewal and FUN!

In London, we stayed with Shalita's cousin Keith, his wife, Ethel, and their three boys. We marveled at the history and explored with Keith and Ethel as our guides. We then spent a few days in the quaint city of Bath before heading back to London, and then to Paris. After tromping around Paris we then ventured south to the lovely city of Blois in the Loire Valley. It was during our time in France when Shalita felt a nudging from God to leave Sierra College.

When we returned home, she put out some feelers and was quickly hired at Cal State University, Sacramento (CSUS). The new job couldn't have come at a better time and it was a welcome change. She loved being part of the university and the new environment. But while she was glad to escape the drama, acrimony, and finger pointing at Sierra College, she felt deeply hurt by the whole experience. Shalita had always envisioned leaving Sierra with a celebration that included her many colleagues and friends. Instead, the two of us went to her office on campus one evening and boxed up all of her personal things and took them home. That was it. After eleven years, she slipped quietly away at night, and the thought of leaving the college under such a dark cloud disgusted her.

July 30, 2001
What do you want to bless me in? You have already given me so much and yet I know and believe that you will bless me in my job at CSUS. You will use me – you will bless me as a wife and mother, as a daughter, sister and friend. Please use me and bless me with strength, peace and unwavering dependence on You. Encourage me Lord and use me greatly. Lord, I specifically ask for justice at Sierra College regarding my case. I have been wrongly accused and slandered and the false findings have tarnished my name. Lord I specifically ask for a blessing here.

She went on to ask God that the truth be brought to light and that her name be cleared. She also asked to be led to a strong, ethical attorney to fight her case. She began to talk with attorneys about a potential lawsuit against the college and eventually went with a partner at her attorney's law firm. Steve was a tall, amiable man with a welcoming smile. A Christian, in his late fifties, Steve was interested in the case, and we both felt like he would pursue the case against Sierra College aggressively and with integrity. He agreed to take on the case.

Shalita was energized by the lawsuit. She was certain that the truth would emerge and paint a different picture, a more truthful story of both what really happened with the tenure committees and how the college wrongly turned on her. Her friends encouraged her to pursue the lawsuit. While I initially supported the idea of a lawsuit, it wasn't long before I could see the cost of pursuing legal recourse against the college. When institutions are sued, not unlike when someone is attacked, they fight back. And Sierra College fought back aggressively. The college had recently settled a suit against them on a human resource issue and they weren't about to settle quickly or be taken to court without a fight.

The lawsuit consumed Shalita, both in terms of time and emotion. When I discussed the toll it was taking on her and our family, she felt hurt. She took my comments to mean that I wasn't supporting her, which was not the case; however, I could see where this was headed. I foresaw the stress of reliving all the painful events of the past two years at Sierra was evident, and it troubled me.

Over the course of the first year of the lawsuit, she spent hundreds of hours compiling documents and retracing events over the last few years. I quietly hoped that a friend would pull her aside and say, "Look, you have every right to be angry at the college, but you need to let go of this and move on because it's hurting you." But that didn't happen. She felt compelled to give the suit her all, and the emotional cost was considerable.

The worst thing about the case was Shalita being interrogated by the college's attorney. She was called to answer questions from the college's counsel and it was extremely stressful and made her even angrier. She bitterly resented it. While she had been the one to file the lawsuit against unfair and inappropriate tactics by college administration, she found herself under attack and had to defend herself from the torrent of questions and accusations. It didn't help that we were dealing with several other issues of health in the family, including my own.

May 26, 2003

I start this journal on a sunny May morning. It is 8 am and I have been awake for 2 hours while my family sleeps. A quiet house . . . all I hear are the birds outside. It is peaceful and it is in this quietness and peace that I run to my Savior Jesus longing for a deep infilling of His mighty power. I am in a battlefield. It has been a war zone all week with my lawsuit – grueling 8-hour depositions, Bill's illness, Mom B's deteriorating condition, Dryw's accident – broken elbow, lacerations, emergency room. I know that my battles are not against flesh and blood but against forces of darkness beyond my vision. But I cling to my Jesus because He is greater than all around me and infinitely more powerful. I am yet reminded again that I am on holy ground even in the battlefield. And it is in this quiet moment I release my fears, anxieties, hopes, desires, frustration, anger and sadness to you, Jesus. Lighten my load Lord, give me the rest and peace that you promise. Make me a faithful soldier and a courageous warrior. This is your battle, Lord . . .

After more than a year of work and anguish, the lawsuit was settled. Once Shalita's attorney took out his fees, which were modest, Shalita was awarded a small sum, amounting to less than two months pay. It was a joke. Given the hours she put into the case, it would probably have been equivalent to minimum wage or less. Not only was the money far short of what she had hoped for, the suit did little to achieve one of her main goals—to clear her name. Furthermore, as a condition of the settlement, the college made her sign a contract that prevented her from ever applying for future employment within the district.

For Shalita it was more than a battle to clear her name or to seek justice for those who were dishonest. Growing up on a campus, and coming from a family steeped in the honorable pursuit of truth and knowledge, it had bigger implications. For Shalita it was ultimately about maintaining high academic standards. It was about ensuring that students have the best academic and educational experience possible. And it was about holding management accountable for retaliating on her when she tried to speak the truth.

Shalita's long journey at Sierra College was over. While she had made wonderful, lifelong friends and touched hundreds of students in the eleven years she taught there, the last few years had been costly and the lawsuit represented a disappointing conclusion.

***

As the lawsuit began winding down, my mother's health began to decline. In 2003, my mom was in her eighties and, although we didn't know it immediately, she began experiencing mini strokes, called TIAs (transient ischemic attacks). These small strokes would come on quickly and were often not recognizable to her or to others around her. While not as damaging or dangerous as a full stroke, the result is a progressive deterioration in the person's physical and cognitive function, as was the case with my mom. This was hard for all of our family to witness, especially my father. Both my parents were fiercely independent and didn't want to "bother" my siblings or me. For months, my parents shrugged off offers of help until the situation developed into a crisis. Mom was in and out of the hospital and my dad finally agreed to get help with her care at home.

For my dad, it was a very difficult transition from what he had known. Used to having his meals served to him, he went from the traditional, "Where's dinner?" to becoming the primary caregiver for Mom. Dad had been through many difficult times in his life, including being a prisoner in Germany during World War II, yet he described the decline in Mom's health as the most difficult thing he ever had to deal with. My two sisters and I tried our best to help, but it was difficult and emotionally taxing. In particular, my father relied on me for advice and assistance with setting up care for mom. This was no easy task, as he drove away several of the women that came to care for Mom, I'm convinced, with his demands and occasional emotional outbursts. Shalita's father, too, was experiencing some difficult health issues.

I was stressed and exhausted. Along with my ongoing back and joint pain, I experienced episodes of extreme fatigue, which sometimes lasted for days. My work responsibilities also changed as I took on a new assignment to be the office lead on a new high-profile agency-wide report. I recall feeling like I didn't have a good grasp of the new project and it added another layer of stress to my already hectic life. In May 2003 I left work early one day because I experienced something for the first time—an intense panic attack.

I was talking with a colleague on the third floor of my building, and we were standing next to a rail that looked over a large atrium. As we talked, seemingly out of nowhere, I had this terrifying thought of jumping over the rail. From where I was, probably fifty feet above the ground floor, jumping would have meant certain death. Two sides of my mind battled against each other and I was paralyzed. *What is going on?* I thought. While I nodded my head as if to listen to my colleague, I was completely oblivious to what he was saying. This was not something I had ever experienced. It was torture trying to calm down and figure out how to politely extricate myself away from the railing. When I got back to my desk I knew that something was seriously wrong with my mind and I went home. I took off a few days of work and immediately started counseling to try to clear my head and figure out what was going on.

Somewhere, deep in the recesses of my brain, it was as if a circuit had blown. While I couldn't see it at the time, it was the first big clue that I my body was saying, *There's too much on your plate!* I didn't understand what had happened and it frightened me. This was the beginning of many similar episodes in which I no longer felt comfortable with heights.

In August 2003, we moved from Rocklin to Carmichael, an established community closer to both of our jobs and to our parents. By that fall Shalita and I were both feeling weary. The lawsuit, moving, and health issues with our parents all took a toll on us. On a whim I searched the web for fares to Paris, to make good on our dream to travel there, just the two of us. We made a quick plan for a romantic, weeklong getaway.

November 8, 2003

On board United Airlines. In less than an hour we will be landing in Paris. It is still unreal that Bill and I are making this trip together without our boys. It is a gift from God and so desperately needed. This has been such a difficult year for both of us dealing with Bill's health, Mom B's rapid decline, Dad's illness. The nightmarish lawsuit with Sierra, which is thankfully behind us, the move to (Carmichael), change, growth and more life issues. We are both physically, emotionally and mentally spent and stressed out. We so need to reconnect.

In His infinite grace and tenderness, God worked out this trip at the most unlikely time for me – the middle of a semester. Things fell into place – great airfares, free nights at the Hilton in Paris . . .

Up to the last minute I wasn't sure about going. A week ago my beloved Dad collapsed and was rushed to the hospital – 5 days there and is now home. Even in the emergency room, he said not to cancel the trip – I had so much apprehension about leaving him and have released it to God and know that he is in God's hands, as are Mum, the boys and the rest of the family. I also commit Mom B. to Jesus. She was moved to a nursing home last week, fell and received stitches. It is heartbreaking to see her condition and to feel Bill's pain. It has been so hard for us to see our parents age and deal with the hardships of aging – their frailties, dependency and pain. It makes me afraid of aging and makes me so aware of my mortality and the purpose of my life . . .

This visit to Paris is so significant for a couple of reasons. The first is that it was during our visit to Paris in 2001 that I had my epiphany – the clear direction from the Lord to leave Sierra College. On our return home after the trip, I resigned from a job that I thought I would retire from and that had complete financial security. The world of CSUS opened up – less pay and security – but infinitely more positive, nurturing, as well as challenging. So in some ways my trip back is a full circle of victory!

The other reason is that last time our trip was too brief and with the boys – even though it was wonderful and memorable, we never got to do the adult fun stuff – museums and shopping ☺ we wanted to do. So this is our dream trip because we always talked about coming here together without the kids.

With the exception of a brief business trip I had to Vancouver, British Columbia, traveling to Paris was the only international trip we took without the kids. This time we visited the Louvre, Musée d'Orsay, and Versailles. We marveled at the gargoyles outside Notre Dame, we hiked to the top of the Arc de Triomphe at night, we strolled along the Champs-Élysées, acting shocked at the high prices.

The first night in our Hilton Hotel (La Defense), neither of us could sleep, and we felt the curse of flying over the Atlantic. We loved the mattress, much different to what we were used to in the US. At two in the morning we talked and talked and eventually fell asleep.

The weather was crisp but not too cold, and we were two tourists glad to escape the trials that had engulfed us at home. One of our joys was coming back to the hotel for the evening after a long day of sightseeing and shopping, where we were happily greeted by the staff, "Bonjour Mr. and Mrs. Blackburn, did you enjoy your day?" We loved it! They quickly broke the stereotype of unfriendly Parisians and made our stay as sweet as could be. It was a slice of heaven and we soaked it up. Even the flight home was delightful (as delightful as you can be in coach at 38,000 feet). One of the flight attendants remembered us from the trip from San Francisco a week earlier. She spoiled us. "Would you like some champagne, we have some extra from first class? And here are some extra travel kits, if you would like them." We mostly enjoyed talking with her and getting the perspective of a profession far different from either of ours.

Regretfully, there was one evening on our trip when we fought over Shalita's penchant for buying things, gifts for friends mostly. She was so mad at my insensitive comment that she told me she would go home early without me! I was foolish and regretted it immediately.

But one tiff did not mar the otherwise perfect trip. We both needed to get away and the seven nights in Paris were a gift to us.

Chapter 8

Something's Not Right

Numerous life events had taken a heavy toll on Shalita. In the legal battle with Sierra College, she felt that her attorney had settled for far too little. She hated the idea that she had been forced out and that, instead of clearing her name and being compensated for the unethical and highly unusual events that had occurred under the president's tenure, the suit had accomplished very little. It was also hard adjusting to our new community of Carmichael, as we struggled to care for our parents. As my mother continued to decline in late 2003, she caught pneumonia in the nursing home and died in January 2004. It was painful for all of the family to see Mom's passing. While I felt blessed that I had grown up with such a loving and warm mother, the ache of losing her was deep. It was a mentally and physically exhausting season for us.

In April 2004, I remember Shalita saying she felt poorly. She often felt fatigued and told me that she felt "something was just not right." While there was nothing acute or obviously wrong, she sensed something was going on inside of her—her body was whispering subtle clues to her, *but what did it mean*? She saw her physician, Dr. Teymouri, and he ordered several standard tests. A few things of concern were found, but nothing serious—high cholesterol and a troubling enzyme reading with her liver, as I recall.

In June, Shalita and her sister-in-law Deana traveled to Washington DC for a week. She looked forward to spending time with Deana and seeing two of her cousins that lived in the area. She wanted to get away from the many demands at home too. Her emotional and physical wellbeing were being taxed and spiritually she struggled, as evidenced in her journal entries. In the second paragraph she refers to the Apostle Paul and how in Romans 7:15 he acknowledges his human weaknesses and writes, "I do not understand what I do. For what I want to do I do not do, but what I hate I do."

June 24, 2004

Today is a beginning of a journey away from my family for a week. Away from Bill and the boys, pressures of keeping all the balls in air and trying to balance everyone's needs. So much has happened in the past year leaving me weary. I feel deadness in my spirit and I desperately need to look inside and rebuild my relationship with God. Never have I felt so distant in my spirit from God, yet I know He is with me. I have been in a desert for far too long. My vision is clouded and so many feelings overwhelm me. I see joy, hope and peace on the other side, but a chasm of anger and unforgiveness separates me. Sometimes the hurt of anger, or anger of being hurt feels brittle and so foreign.

I hate what it is doing to me – my marriage and peace of mind. It has zapped my energy – physically my body screams – migraines, chest pains. I know what the Psalmist prayed when he talked of the weariness in his bones and the tears. I need to be cleansed from my core – healed, renewed and given a purpose. Only God can do this miracle. I feel even some of my anger is directed at God and for this I am ashamed deeply for how I dare to be angry at God who has given Himself freely to me. I know the demons I face are spiritual – fear, doubt, pride, insecurity – I cannot see a clear vision and purpose unless I confess my anger and hurt to God and beg on my knees for forgiveness and healing. I have tried on my own and failed. I am filled with loathing at the fruit of my anger and resentment – hurtful unkind words, desire to hurt and retaliate, pride, the need to prove myself – the need to control events – not giving others the benefit of doubt. It is an ugly picture of my heart. Who am I? I belong to Jesus. I yearn to do right, to serve Him to be a light and blessing and yet I am torn inside. Is this how Paul felt? I want to do the things that are good and yet the greatest battle I fight is within.

Lord, I want to come back to you and it goes deeper than wanting – I <u>need</u> to be restored to come back to you. Even more than I need air to breathe. My spirit is suffocated with sin. Breathe your spirit in me. Please forgive me Father. I am so sorry and unworthy. Please God, I want the sweetness, the fragrance of Jesus to infuse me – the forgiveness of the Father, the power and strength of the Holy Spirit to renew me and give me a clear vision.

Father God you are my judge and my creator. I am so afraid of living an unfulfilled life – of dying and not being ready to meet you because I was not a faithful steward of what you entrusted to me on this earth – time, money, energy, talent. So much . . . Jesus, my Redeemer, I know that in the end all I do will be worthless because only your Blood has cleansed and redeemed me and that is my own claim to salvation. Holy Spirit – I have grieved you by pushing you away – not allowing you to work because of my desire to control. Please heal me . . .

Forgive me for not seeing the good in those who have hurt me – not seeing how much you have given me and how much I need to be thankful, Jesus. I am journeying into my soul and cannot do it and expect to have clarity unless you forgive, heal and remove these weights around my neck. I do not want to return to Sacramento the same person – I want my family to see a new me because of You.

Rekindle your fire in me – I want to fall in love with you all over again and with my husband, my kids and my life. Please renew and reestablish my priorities. I cannot live a moment longer without communing with You. Seal the door on past hurts and regrets, Lord, please let me grow and learn from them. Fill me with joy and peace. Release the chains that tie me and only make me a captive for you.

Please watch over Bill this week and my boys. Renew Bill's heart too Lord. Soften him, deepen his faith and encourage him. Protect him and my precious boys – Dryw and Daniel – keep them safe. Please watch over Dad and Mum and John.

I pray for a special and memorable time for Deana and me. Please deepen our relationship. Keep me from being impatient.

Bless our time with Averil and Charlene. Let this trip bring healing and peace and deepen love and understanding to everyone. Solidify our family please. Also God, please let Averil and Charlene see you in me and Deana – in our relationship and our conversation.

Thank you for the gift of this trip to Washington DC. The excitement and promise of the time ahead and most of all for this time to reflect and think and journey close to you. Lord please show me how you want me to live my life. I want to spend time with you every day. Teach me lessons from your word – speak to me clearly so I can understand.

Thank you Lord I feel your touch and healing as I write. I feel you smile and my soul smiles. I'm back in your arms – keep me there please – always . . .

Shalita came home excited about her time with her cousins and seeing her relationship with her sister-in-law Deana grow ever stronger. But she also came home very physically tired.

In early August, we traveled to Oregon with the boys for a family vacation. I have happy memories of walking around downtown Portland, looking out at the awesome Oregon coast and enjoying ice cream at Tillamook creamery. Soon after we returned home from Oregon, Shalita began to complain that she didn't feel well. On Sunday, August 15th, we went out to lunch after church and Shalita complained of abdominal pain. Later that day, she showed me that her entire abdominal area was bloated. I didn't think too much about it, and figured she was retaining water or something similar.

On Monday morning she made an appointment with her doctor, Dr. Teymouri, and was able to get in the next day. Because her doctor was unavailable, she saw a female physician in the office. When she complained about her discomfort and extended abdomen she was prescribed a diuretic to reduce fluid buildup. Shalita was troubled and questioned the prescription of a diuretic. She called her brother Chris, an oncologist. Hearing her symptoms Chris immediately became concerned that her problem had been misdiagnosed. He called Dr. Teymouri's office and strongly suggested she get a CT scan as soon as possible. Her doctor agreed, and she had the scan the next day, Wednesday. In addition, her doctor's office ordered a procedure to have the abdominal fluid removed. On Thursday, I went with her to the appointment. A very long needle was inserted to her abdomen to remove the fluid. The procedure was very painful and she moaned through much of it. I recall them showing us a glass container filled with about a quart of cloudy fluid they had removed. This made both of us uncomfortable. *What had caused the fluid? What did this mean?* The specimen was sent to the lab.

Based on their estimate, we were to hear the results of the lab test either the following day, Friday, or possibly Monday. On Friday, Shalita had an existing appointment with her OB/GYN doctor and discussed her concerns over the developing situation. Her OB/GYN doctor thought it could be one of three things, including the possibility that she could have ovarian cancer. Shalita was very upset at the news, but I think we both believed in our hearts there had to be a good explanation of what was occurring and that in the end it wouldn't be serious. The weekend dragged on, and while we prayed and prayed for a favorable outcome, we were both anxious about the lab test.

Monday finally came. August 23rd. Shalita had asked me to stay home from work so that we could hear the news about the lab report together. I somewhat reluctantly agreed to stay home, my mind convinced that the news would be good and we could put this brief period of worry behind us. When the call from Dr. Teymouri's office came, I was balancing the checkbook, half lost in the responsibilities of the day. It was a call that changed our lives.

Twelve months later Shalita recounted the day, as well as the next one.

August 23, 2005
A year ago today I was diagnosed with ovarian cancer. How well I remember that day. Feeling sick all weekend – 9 am Dr. Teymouri's call, "I'm sorry to tell you the tests showed a definite malignancy." Cancer – the dreaded C word had invaded my world and life as I knew it would never be the same. The first steps in a long journey. Chris's call immediately following – "I'll be there." Walking in a daze all day. Too sick to go with Daniel to his first day of school.

Kicked into autopilot – laundry, straightening Daniel's room, anything to bring semblance of normalcy. Packed a bag for the hospital knowing instinctively I would not be coming home that evening. Set out Daniel's clothes for the week. I remember thinking of that line from "Hunt for Red October" where Sam Neil's character says, as he is dying "I would have liked to have seen Montana." Praying loud and crying with Bill – shock, disbelief – life held in suspension. Knowing the only way to move forward – throwing myself into the arms of Jesus to hold and carry me. 3 pm – met with Dr. Rosenberg at Sutter Cancer Center. His manner was clinical, blunt with no warmth. Hearing him talk about surgery, chemotherapy – my mind not comprehending what my ears were hearing. "I'm not going to lie to you – short term prognosis looks good, long term not good." Could this be happening to me? At 45 – looking at my mortality square in the face.

Deana trying to hold it together in front of us. God's hand holding us – wrapped tightly in his hands and arms – so scared. Feeling sicker. "A bed just became available." Wheeled across the hospital – onto the 4th floor "Oncology" – new word – new club to which I was unwillingly initiated. Tears, fears – A nurse came to me "My name is Helen and I am going to take good care of you." Beautiful loving Christian – checked into a bed – phone calls – trying to arrange the week for Daniel from my bed – schedule lessons – Barbara D. sweet dear friend coming and helping out. Talking with Kim – crying – Linda, Clare – My precious Bill.

Dan and Linda coming over in the evening. Dan rubbing my feet – their presence. Dad and Mum there – Dr. Owens walking in. "Mrs. Blackburn, I was expecting someone much older." Holding my hand the whole time he explained the surgery to me. Falling asleep knowing I was in the arms of Jesus and that God was bigger than any of this.

Still trying to absorb the shock of the devastating diagnosis on that hot August day, I remember Shalita asking Dr. Rosenberg if she would see her boys graduate from high school. A short, balding man of about sixty, Rosenberg was all business.

"How old are they?" he asked. "Seven and seventeen," she replied. And then, without pause he shot back: "you'll see the older one graduate."

The realization of what he had said began to sink in, and before we could fully take in this overwhelming news we'd heard, Rosenberg continued. "Look, I don't like to sugar coat it"—a massive understatement—"the odds of surviving five years for ovarian cancer patients at your stage are one in four." *Oh my God, I am going to lose her.* Waves of disbelief and terror washed over me. The news reverberated inside my head and as I tried to grapple with the sudden blackness of our future, I heard Deana begin to weep. Shalita, like me, looked stunned. As Deana's crying continued, I remember thinking, *Pull it together Deana, you're not helping Shalita.* But for Deana, a strong woman and a hospice nurse, the news was too much.

For the second time that day we received news that shattered the world we knew. As I tried to comfort Shalita, I kept thinking, *I am going to lose my precious wife. How could this be?*

After the appointment with Dr. Rosenberg we were sent to admissions and Shalita was immediately admitted to the hospital. That afternoon I stepped outside the hospital and called Chris on my cell phone. The conversation was factual. I explained what was going on now, what Rosenberg had told us. When I hung up I thought, *Is this really happening?* It seemed surreal. It was like a part of my brain accepted the information as fact, but another part of my brain, the emotional side, was taking it in one tiny piece at a time, as if the sink was full but the drain was clogged and the water was draining one drop at a time.

I stayed at the hospital until late that evening. Utterly exhausted, I drove home. Before heading to bed I jumped in the shower. There I tried to process the day's horrible news and what it all meant. Strangely, in the next moment I realized how truly fortunate I was. As if someone had opened my eyes I thought about what an incredible woman Shalita was. It was as if God were saying, *"Bill, I have been trying to tell you this, but you were too busy with life, you were too busy nitpicking and complaining about this and that to know and fully understand what an amazing partner I gave to you."* It took a catastrophic illness and shattering the notion of us growing old together for me to see things clearly. Whatever time we had together, I vowed to spend it fully living and loving each other. What a fool I had been.

The next day was her surgery, and I arrived back at the hospital late morning. Shalita and I talked and prayed between visits with several friends and family that came by. One of the visitors was Deana's brother Marty. As Shalita laid in her hospital bed, Marty shared his own experience with cancer, as well as another life-threatening condition he had faced and explained that God was bigger than anything life can throw at you, including the diagnosis she received the day before. From that, *God is bigger* became her mantra, telling friends and family that came to see her. It was an important expression of faith, but more it was a tangible way to bring perspective to this very scary thing called cancer. Claiming "God is bigger" helped us both let go of some of the fear, because cancer is no match for the Creator of the universe, our loving Father, the Ultimate Healer.

Shalita's surgeon, Dr. Jay Owens, was a big, imposing man. He had a reputation as a gifted surgeon, and his demeanor was warm and comforting, a welcome contrast to Dr. Rosenberg. The surgery was around eight o'clock that evening, and as the time approached I was more than a little nervous of the outcome. *What will they find? What if there are complications?* I had to give this surgery to God. As the surgery began, friends and family grew into to a small crowd as they came to the hospital to support us.

I remember making small talk with my dad and a good friend, Dave Robertson. It was a welcome distraction. The hours went by slowly, painfully so. Finally, at a few minutes before eleven p.m., Dr. Owens came to the waiting area. "The surgery went well and she is doing fine in the recovery room." I felt a huge relief. He said he was able to remove all the cancerous tissue and that her cancer was considered stage IIIC. Stage IIIC was a term that meant nothing to me at the time. I had no point of reference to compare it to. Soon afterward I would become aware of the four stages, with "C" being more advanced than IIIA or IIIB. As the doctors expected, the cancer was fairly advanced, although at least it wasn't stage IV.

As a group we all felt a huge feeling of relief that the surgery had been successful and was over. One by one, everyone left. But I was determined to see her after she was moved from recovery to the intensive care unit. I was told it would be an hour or so before I could see her. All alone and exhausted, hours slowly passed and there was still no word from the nurses about when they would move her to a room and when I could see her. I tried to rest and get a few minutes of sleep in one of the waiting areas outside the ICU. At the time I was suffering from a sore left shoulder, and I couldn't get comfortable. Lying down on the bank of hospital chairs left me uncomfortable and restless.

By two a.m. I became worried that something might be wrong because they still had not moved her and I hadn't received any news on her condition for a few hours. Finally, at 2:45 a.m., they moved her to a room in the ICU and I was able to see her. She was connected to several tubes and wires with machines monitoring her and the ever-present beeps and alarms that occupy ICUs. She was awake but was unable to open her eyes. She asked me how the surgery went and I told her it went well and what Dr. Owens had told us about removing all the cancerous tissue. In my exhausted and anxious state, I began to cry. It was a combination of relief that the procedure had gone well and that I was finally able to see her. But my emotional response worried her. "What's wrong?" she said. "What did Dr. Owens really say?" "That's it, he said the surgery went fine and he got it all," I explained. "You're doing good," I tried to reassure her. Still worried, she continued: "Really, tell me, did he really get it all?"

It was a few more worried moments before I was able to convince her that I wasn't hiding terrible news about her condition. My tears were a mix of joy and relief. Seeing her after this major operation capped two extremely intense days. By 3:30 a.m., I was exhausted. I kissed her goodbye, walked briskly to my car, went home, and collapsed into bed.

August 24, 2005
A year to the date of surgery. Thank you Father for carrying me in your arms this past year – for guiding the hands of Dr. Owens to remove the tumor from my body – for all the multitude of prayers offered for my healing – for your grace and mercy that upheld me and for revealing your power and glory through my healing. I praise and bless you Lord. Please keep my heart fixed on you and looking forward. I thank you

Lord with my whole heart for healing me. I remember waking up early (the day of the surgery) to see Deana sitting in the dark across from me praying for me – No breakfast – Having to drink lots of yucky stuff to make me poop ☺ and purge my insides.

Marty coming over in the morning praying for me. Saying "God is bigger." Later Eileen, Tom Savage and Ed Donahue coming to pray over me and anoint me with oil. Roselene and Clare with me as part of the circle of prayer. Believing God was bigger than the cancer. Dan and Linda coming over – moving to a private room – Being able to laugh with Linda in the midst of all this. Mum and Dad, Dryw, Bill, John and Deana, Cal and Nancy praying with me – Surgery ahead of schedule – the guys from OR came early – feeling the fear and panic and praying "Jesus hold me." Bill with me going to the surgery. Cold sterile room – clinging to Bill's hand – saying goodbye and then into the operating room – leaning forward into the nurse's arm while they put me asleep and then oblivion. Waking up and calling for Bill – His tears – Oh thank you Jesus. My heart is too full for words, my spirit rejoices for you.

Chapter 9

Treating Body and Soul

With the surgery behind us, we could focus on the next stage—chemotherapy. Before we knew it, we were thrust into a new paradigm, a new world. While Shalita was still in the hospital recovering from surgery, they started her on chemotherapy, with the strategy of beginning it as soon as possible. Starting treatment just a few days after surgery, we had little time to absorb what this diagnosis really meant.

September 20, 2004
'The test showed malignancy – you have cancer.' With those words the normal world as I knew it shattered and from then on my life would be divided into two segments – 'Before I had cancer' to 'Now I have cancer.' Someday it will be a trilogy with the finale 'when I had cancer' and yet as I write I focus on the long difficult journey I face. I cannot walk this path alone – ahead lies uncertainty, fear, pitfalls, demons of doubt and insecurity and I know that I must and need to place my hand in Jesus – as a trusting child walking behind Him as He leads me upward, downward, forward and sideways through a narrow twisted path. He is the light and that keeps the night from being complete blackness to me and he has given me a small lamp to guide each step – one at a time. The lamp I carry is not a beacon that would light the whole way. No, the lamp given me is small but enough to light the path ahead of my steps. To keep me from stumbling over my feet or (tripping) over a rock. I can only step knowing that Jesus my light and beacon is walking ahead of me – clearing the rough spots, removing boulders – working unseen miracles and He is and knows my journey's end.

As I walk I am surrounded from all sides by faithful prayer warriors and supporters cheering me on, encouraging me to stand up when I falter, to strengthen my resolve when it is weak. They are an army headed by my husband and precious life partner Bill, my boys Dryw and Daniel, my life givers through Jesus, Dad and Mum, my beloved brothers . . . I see my Linda closer than a sister – screaming for victory, Kim and so many, many others through that path.

And I know that with all this support and God's Word that has promised me "The Lord will heal all your diseases" – Exodus 15:26 "That I must move forward and with my head up in courage and determination."

With God's help, I will not let this disease rob me of the precious life God has given me. With God's healing, it will not rob my children of their mother, my Bill of his wife and my family of their daughter, sister and aunt. My heart is at peace with God – my salvation is secure in Him. He and I know that. But there is too much unfinished business and work for me in this life – now. I pray for time. I am not a statistic and God is bigger than any stages of cancer or prognosis. As God is my witness I will have victory in Him over this disease. People and doctors will be amazed and God's healing power and majesty will be glorified by everyone.

As I sit here receiving my second cycle of chemo I see each day as God's healing oil entering my body and killing the bad cells and strengthening the new ones.

God is God. He is to be uplifted always – I am in your hands, dear Lord. Amen

Shalita's chemotherapy was administered over a three-week cycle. A few days after her infusions she would feel the worst— nausea, fatigue, achiness throughout much of her body. Carboplatin was the chemo drug she received. The chemo, of course, targeted fast-growing cells, including cancerous cells, but also had the effect of killing hair follicles. While Shalita came home from the hospital thin and weak, she looked good and had a full head of hair. We knew it was very likely she would lose it, and before long her thick, beautiful hair began to fall like waves of pouring rain. Despite knowing that the hair loss was coming, it was a depressing, painful process for her.

When faced with so many aspects of life that were out of her control, ones she had taken for granted until then, she grabbed the reins and decided she would do what she could. She rummaged through the hall closet one day and pulled out an electric razor. Walking over to me she said, "Bill, I want you to cut my hair before it all falls out." I looked up at her sensing the emotional struggle inside of her. I took the razor and together we walked into the master bathroom. Spreading a bath towel on the ground, she stepped on it and I began the unpleasant task of giving her my attempt at a crew cut. Large clumps came out and we suffered together as her head took on its new bare shape.

I don't remember what happened next; we hugged, I think. Over the next few weeks the short hairs she still had found their way onto her pillow, her sweaters, and down the bath drain. In time her eyebrows and eyelashes too were gone. The chemo, as it was intended, was poisoning her, and as it attacked any remnant cancerous cells that were not removed during surgery, she suffered the many effects.

As winter approached and the temperature dropped, one day I noticed Shalita's nose was running a lot. She was constantly wiping her nose with a tissue. At first we thought the runny nose might have been caused by the chemo, but we soon realized that it was because all the little hairs in her nose had fallen out, like the rest of her hair.

September 27, 2004
A week after my 2nd cycle – Hard, hard week last week with nausea, fatigue. Christine's visit a breath of sunshine – her angelic presence – like having both Chris and Deb here.

A new morning, a new week. Two more weeks till my 3rd cycle. I'll be half way done then. I focus every ounce of energy on walking the path of letting God heal me. This is the ultimate battle of my life and with God's help I will be victorious . . .

September 30, 2004
Yesterday was a good day and so is today! I feel more energy, hope and normal. My blood count (CBC) was normal. Lord I feel your awesome healing at work in my body. Heal me Jesus – fulfill your purpose in my life Father. Heal my mind, heart and soul too for it has a cancer of its own. Leftover hurts, grudges, pain. Jesus I release to you all the hurts in my life – justified and unjustified. They weigh me down. Forgive me for not letting go of these – for hanging on to past grievances.

November 11, 2004
A better week. Last Thurs., Fri., and Sat. were the worst ever – I felt hit by a fleet of trucks that ran over me then reversed and hit me again – severe nausea and vomiting, yuck. Bill's birthday was a downer physically but he went out with Dad B. to Apple Hill, etc. – I'm glad at least it wasn't totally rotten for him. Mum was here till Sat. All I could do was lay my head on her lap. Finally, Chris figured out it was the Effexor Dr. R put me on – Way too strong – 75 mg! Should have started out with 25 mg! Chris is brilliant and so sweet. Finally felt better on Sunday evening. Weak on Mon., drove to Target and could barely make it out – shakes and cold sweat. Tues. and Wed. better. Did a lot of stuff around the house – laundry, cleaned closet.

I record all my symptoms in detail so that when this is over I will never forget how awful this is physically (did I mention the awful taste in my mouth – bitter and metallic? I also developed neuroma on my fingers – tingling. Cold and hot flashes, sweats, unbearable itching on my back, sides of feet and palms). My body has been beaten up. I write this not to complain but to keep myself in touch with this experience so I can have greater compassion and sensitivity to others going through this and when this is over (2 more sessions) I can draw on this to help and minister to others. This is a fiery furnace.

There are endless times when all I can do is cry to God 'You are my stronghold, Jesus hold me, get me through this,' and he has never failed me. I can't wait to testify what God is doing and will do through this situation. I see how His hand has worked, how He planned each detail. I will emerge from this a new person. Teach me to number my days aright that I may gain a heart of wisdom, Oh God. Melt and mold me. You have stripped me of all externals, roles of being total mom and wife, independence, job title, even physical appearance (I'm bald under a great wig thanks to Evelyn), my eyelashes are sparse. I don't recognize me in the mirror when I step out of the shower. Yet Lord I am still me – the one you love – you cherish me enough to die for – I'm thankful Lord for life – for being here.

During August and early September, my schedule became a long series of trips running back and forth to Sutter General Hospital. In time I knew every hallway and exit at Sutter. It became routine. Exit J Street off westbound Capital City Freeway. Cross 29th street and turn left into the parking lot under the freeway. Sneak across 29th street, into the hospital, and jog up the stairs to the fourth floor. Mentally I would brace myself for whatever news I might hear when I got there. I would try to bolster myself to be upbeat, fighting the natural ache I felt inside from watching Shalita struggle to recover from her surgery and then immediately begin chemotherapy. The hospital runs became rote, both oddly comforting knowing I would see my lovely wife, and depressing, seeing the dimly lit road ahead.

One of the things I've learned from the many times of having family in the hospital is the importance of being vigilant about making sure the medical staff is providing excellent care. I quickly learned how important it was to closely monitor Shalita's care. Keeping an eye on the medical staff was absolutely critical, and I found that by asking questions, especially of the ever-present nurses, I would often catch a problem before it became more serious. After many days of visiting Shalita, I knew the nurses by name and they knew me. Most were excellent and our family was pleased to see them taking good care of her. Some, however, were less competent or were difficult to work with. By staying on top of her condition, her medications, and asking a lot of questions, I was confident that Shalita was receiving excellent care.

In early September, as she healed from the surgery and I had less to worry about, I took to the internet, and like many in my situation, I researched this dreaded disease. Understanding that the odds of Shalita living a normal full life were not in our favor, I tried to take in all I could about the disease and to find ways to lower the risk of recurrence. Over the next few months I researched aggressively. Some of the information I found was encouraging, however, some stirred up fears and was hard to read. Mostly, it was a way for me, and for us, to regain some control. Shalita's diagnosis of cancer was beyond our control and it was life threatening. While we had dozens of families and friends praying for Shalita's recovery, we were going to do all we could to keep her healthy.

For me this obsession ran its course. After a few months of searches and visits to the library, I had learned a lot about ovarian cancer and the importance of strengthening the immune system—the body's natural way of fighting disease, including cancer. Some of the information that Shalita and I learned was helpful and we did our best to implement them. But I began to realize several important things. First, all the knowledge in the world would not guarantee that Shalita would "beat" cancer and live a long and healthy life. Second, I had limited time to research all the possible cures. After all, I had to continue working, look after myself, the boys, and help maintain the house without Shalita's help. Third, the decisions on maintaining a healthy lifestyle and future treatment were ultimately Shalita's choices. While we agreed on most things in this area, Shalita had a strong constitution and wasn't about to do something she didn't agree with, despite my best arguments. For example, in my research some sources described how sugar weakened the immune system. Shalita was a liberal user of sugar in coffee and tea, as well as in her desserts. When I brought that up and tried to get her to reduce her sugar intake, she protested.

One of the things I quickly learned as I began my research is that women diagnosed with ovarian cancer are given a blood test to determine the level of a specific tumor marker—cancer antigen (CA)

125. This protein is found in the bloodstream, and it quickly became a new part of our family's vocabulary. For healthy women, the CA 125 level is below 35 (U/ml). We were told Shalita's CA 125 level initially was sky high, more than 9800. When Chris heard this, he feared the worst, envisioning the surgeon opening Shalita up and finding the cancer spread throughout much of the body. If that were the case, her prognosis would be bleak, with little chance of living more than months or even weeks. While the extremely high tumor marker was a bad sign and the tumor had metastasized from the ovaries to the abdominal cavity, fortunately, it had not spread throughout the rest of her body.

After the surgery Shalita's CA 125 level dropped precipitously to less than 2000. And after her first chemotherapy it dropped again, to less than 100! We were very excited. And over the course of the next few months, we watched and celebrated as it ultimately dropped to single digits. Every few months Shalita would religiously have her CA 125 level checked, and each time we waited on pins and needles to hear the results.

One day, while Shalita was at Sutter Hospital for a doctor's appointment, she was feeling apprehensive and discouraged. She tried to stay positive but it was difficult. Trying to take her mind off of the present worries, she picked up a 2001 issue of *Redbook* magazine in the waiting room. As she thumbed through it she came across an article on the best doctors in the country for treating breast cancer. On the list of the best oncologists, she was excited to see her brother's name, Dr. Christopher Chitambar, from the Medical College of Wisconsin. The pride and admiration she felt was exceeded only by her sense that God had drawn her to that magazine, to that article, and that she was indeed being blessed.

***

In December 2004 Shalita finished her last course of chemotherapy. Her body was weak from the poisoning effects of the drugs. We were all glad it was over. Slowly her strength began to return. Not long after she completed her chemo treatment, Shalita heard about a medical trial for a new drug specifically for ovarian cancer patients.

The study was being conducted at Stanford University Medical Center in the South Bay Area. The drug was called OvaRex. She met all the eligibility requirements to participate in the study, and we both felt it was worth trying. She consulted her oncologist, as well as Chris, and we both prayed about whether or not she should participate. We were told that the odds were two chances in three that she was getting the drug and not the placebo, but of course we didn't know which one she would get. She wanted to participate in the study not only to potentially improve her odds of survival, but she also felt that it was important to help advance the work to ultimately find a cure for this deadly disease.

As if there weren't already enough on our minds, the day we first went to Stanford we returned to find that Shalita's father had suddenly become ill. It wasn't clear initially if it was serious, but because of his heart condition and age, he was admitted to the hospital.

February 6, 2005
Thank you Lord for life and breath – a new month and the promise it brings. You have promised that you will never give us more than we can handle and I cling to that promise Lord. My beloved Dad is in ICU – congestive heart failure resulting in fluid build up in his lungs – he has pneumonia. It is the same ICU ward I was in at Sutter. Was in ER with him till 1 am. I realize I am still traumatized and raw from the whole experience. I couldn't stop shaking – please Lord, I lift my dad to you. Even in the ICU, hooked up to oxygen, with difficultly breathing he said: "you're going to be all right – God has a plan for your life – the best is ahead." Oh Jesus, I know I can't hold on to my parents forever but please Jesus I need him so much right now. Please help Dad make it through this. Help him to see Dryw graduate from high school. Everything is in your hands dear Lord – I trust you.

February 13, 2005
The Hands of My Lord
Psalm 92:4 . . . I sing for joy at the works of your hands.

- Powerful Hands – that created the universe, sun, stars, moons, earth, sky, gave life and breath to all
- Gentle Hands – that held children, blessed them, fed the hungry, touched the sick and maimed, reached out to Peter when he was sinking and grasped him
- Healing Hands – that healed hurt, pain, shame, betrayal, guilt, pride, confusion, disease, renewing life and giving life
- Holy Hands – lifting up to the Father in prayer, blessing the food, breaking the bread, washing the feet of the disciples, raised up to Heaven
- Comforting Hands – crying with Mary and Martha, touching and healing
- Sacrificial Hands – stretched out on the cross for my sins, full of nail prints
- Victorious Hands – blessing His disciples being lifted up to Heaven
- Faithful Arms – holding me "underneath are the everlasting arms" gather me in His arms like a shepherd, leading me and directing me in the way I should go.

Blessed Lord I place myself in your arms – wrap me in them – I claim the power, healing, holiness, comfort, sacrificial love, faithfulness and guidance from you. Please fill and saturate me with the breath of your Holy Spirit. Continue please Lord to renew me – heal me and make me a new person. I worship you for the work of Your Hands in my life – the miracle of your healing.

Jesus please help my beloved Dad pull through this. I know he is in your arms. I plead for his life Lord. Please don't take him yet Lord – we all need him so much and he wants so much to live. Please help his body fight the infection and his lungs to heal. Father, he is safe in you. Keep our faith strong. Please be with Mum especially and strengthen her. Father you know the spoken and the unspoken prayers of my heart. Please comfort and heal my body every day. Please restore my immune system to fight any recurring disease. Protect my sweet husband and boys.

February 15, 2005
Oh the deep, deep love of Jesus – I can't wait to be in your word to sit at your feet. My hunger and thirst for you Lord is insatiable. I have prayed and longed for this Lord – to be, just be in your presence. To know that you understand the deep longing of my spirit – the groans and utterances that go beyond words. I worship and praise you for what you have done in my life these past months. You have healed and transformed me and shown me your power without a shadow of doubt – You are God – your faithfulness knows no bounds. You are eternal and faithful and you keep your promises. Your healing power is awesome. You are an awesome God! Lord I bow down in reverence at your healing power. As I read my journal I am amazed at the journey – at your working and answered prayers. Bless you Lord.

Father I feel your strength in me. I am so sad by Dad's condition in ICU – it breaks my heart but I feel your strength in me, your assurance. I have felt that I have been living at the hospital this past week. I am tired and exhausted, yet I feel your arms holding me close. Jesus I pray for healing for my Dad – you could have not given me a better earthly father – godly, wise, devoted, strong, tender and full of integrity and purpose. Please heal him Lord. We want him to live and he wants to live. We all need him so much.

Father please strengthen my Mum who looks so frail. I give all plans and decisions about their future living arrangements to you. Please be with us all.

Jesus, continue to strengthen my immune system. Bless all the efforts on my part to exercise, rest, eat well and meditate to heal me completely. You are the greatest healer of all Lord – Please heal me completely – despite the stress I am undergoing with Dad. Shield every cell of my body from a recurrence. Protect my body as I honor it as your temple and offer it to you. Make me a good steward. Father please heal my body from the effects of chemo – my bone marrow, WBCs, RBCs, CA 125 – keep it <u>down</u> even thru the study.

My faith is in You Lord, not in OvaRex or anything else. I will do my part Lord to partner with you in protecting my health. Please give me a long and healthy life – to cherish each day with my beloved husband and boys. My purpose is to be wife and mom and to nurture my friendships and reach out for you. Make my life count and make me a blessing.

I give Bill and the boys to you for blessing, protection and healing – as well as the rest of my family.

I love you Lord with all my heart.

***

At someone's suggestion, a few weeks after chemo treatments started, we discussed joining a cancer support group. I searched online for such groups and made a few calls. During one call I made, I was surprised to speak directly to the doctor facilitating the group, Jonathon Hake. The group met weekly at Mercy Hospital in Folsom, about a half hour away. Dr. Hake had a pleasant, easygoing demeanor and invited us to check out the group. It met on Tuesdays at two p.m.

When we arrived, we found a group of mostly women in a circle. I had the usual reservations about talking with strangers about personal issues, but we were warmly greeted, and it didn't take long to feel comfortable. Most of the women had been diagnosed with breast cancer, although a few had other types of cancers. Shalita was the only one with ovarian cancer. We both found the group easy to talk with and sensed that the group would be helpful for us to deal with the myriad worries and tangled-up feelings that were bouncing around our brains as we faced a difficult and uncertain future.

At first I found it a little odd the way the meeting was conducted. After brief remarks from Dr. Hake and introductions, he would pass a rock around the room. When you were handed the rock it was your turn to talk. As a spouse of a cancer patient, I felt awkward at times knowing what to say. But this remarkable group understood well the difficult journey we were on and how cancer not only greatly affects its hosts but also their families. This small support group was caring and remarkably candid. With the predominance of breast cancer, we had more than a few descriptive and often hilarious stories of pre- and post-surgery drama about all things breast-related.

Shalita quickly bonded with several of the women, especially Vicki, a smart, sassy woman from England. The two instantly hit it off, sharing a love of tea and all things British. I think Vicki was not only taken with Shalita's intelligence and charm, but could see that Shalita's diagnosis was a bitter pill to swallow. For Shalita, they were kindred spirits and like so many cancer survivors, became part of a tightly knit club that was incredibly supportive and fiercely loyal to one another. Over the next year and a half, the members of the support group would be one of our biggest allies, and these new friends would drop anything to help us.

Another group that became important to both of us was NOCC, the National Ovarian Cancer Coalition. Because these woman had all been diagnosed with ovarian cancer, it became another very important resource and support for us. Unlike the Mercy cancer support group, NOCC's mission was to educate women on ovarian cancer and to support those newly diagnosed, as well as their families. Rather than regular meetings to discuss day-to-day challenges and fears of living with cancer, this local Sacramento branch was connected to a much larger national body.

Shalita's diagnosis was a massive jolt that changed many aspects of our lives. One of the most significant was Shalita's view of the past and future. After her diagnosis in August 2004, there was "life before cancer" and "life with cancer." The illness also opened her eyes to insights that could not be understood from books or personal stories, but that had to be experienced. And while we can't always pick our paths in life, Shalita wanted not just to live, but to thrive in a new and very powerful way. The diagnosis had shaken us

110

both to our core, and for her especially, there were no second chances and no going back. She quickly got past *God, why me?* Instead, her view became, *I praise you, God, for giving me this day!*

As with most cancer patients, she lived with a strange mixture of tremendous gratitude for today, but tempered with a healthy dose of anxiety for the future. *Will it come back? If so, when? Will it be treatable?* These were things I lived with too. While I obviously didn't experience the sickness, surgery, and brutal treatment as she did, I was certainly thankful for each successful treatment. And I, too, dreaded every office visit and test for fear of a recurrence. As scary as this journey was to me, ultimately I was only a witness to the disease, an observer.

Shalita thought about returning to work at the university, but decided not to. In part this was due to lingering effects of the treatment and "chemo brain." She would say that chemo brain took away her confidence of being able to successfully teach and field questions. She also didn't want the stress associated with work to compromise her already fragile health. As she slowly regained her strength and stamina, she threw herself into being the best mother, wife, daughter, and friend she could be. She wanted to live more deliberately and not just enjoy each sunset, but spend more time with God through devotionals and through serving at church.

Shalita's letter to Daniel

March 2, 2005
Daniel my precious son ~
You light up my life my 8 year old. Each day I spend with you is a gift from God that I cherish. I feel it even more deeply since last August 23rd when I was diagnosed with ovarian cancer. It has been a difficult year for us with my surgery, 2 hospitalizations and chemotherapy. You have been so amazing through all this. When I was really sick from chemo, you would rub my feet and cover me with a blanket. It was hard on you and once you said, "4 months is a long time to wait." I remember one day between treatments I was feeling better and sitting on the recliner. I had just come home from the hospital and you sat on the floor next to me and played with your

blocks. After that you climbed up on my lap and carefully covered us up with a blanket and fell asleep. We took a nap together. It was so precious. You were so gentle in hugging me.

Your 8th birthday was at Chuck E. Cheese and you and your friends had a great time. It was also a good week for me. We had a fun celebration. Thanksgiving was fun too with Uncle Chris and Aunt Deb and the family.

You started piano lessons last fall and are very good. Your favorite piece was "If I were a Rich Man" and you played it over and over and over again! Now it's "Heart and Soul." You are very busy with Kid's Alive program at church, as well as karate. You are now a purple belt!

Now that I am all better you feel you have your mommy back. I am home recovering and my hair is growing back. When I was bald you would stroke and kiss my head and you do that now. I wonder what impact my illness will have on you. I hope you see how God is so faithful and answers prayers.

You are in 2nd/3rd grade combo class and are doing so well. Mr. Werly is your teacher and you really like him. You are calling yourself Dan at school! Willy Ju is your best friend and so is Andrew.

Daniel, you are my reason to fight this disease. I pray that God gives me life to see you grow to be a man and to fill your childhood with wonderful memories. You are so precious to me and I love you with all my heart forever.

Mommy

With the chemotherapy completed, during the first half of 2005 Shalita slowly regained most of her strength and stamina. Her nails returned to normal, her hair grew back slowly, and life began to return to, if not normal, a greater level of normalcy. In May she celebrated her 46th birthday by inviting most of her family and friends to her party. It was a true celebration of recovery, thanksgiving, and life itself. Birthdays had always been important to Shalita, but this one was different and she wasn't going to let it slip by without *fully* celebrating it. The party was at John and Deana's house and most of the guests, nearly all women, each contributed to a scrapbook in Shalita's honor. It was a day I remember well, and she relished it.

July 29, 2005

A new journal – a new phase. As I sit in the quiet tranquility of Barbara Dawson's home, I feel myself unwind and breathe deep within myself. Quiet me Lord to this moment now – to a cancer-free body today only made possible through the miracle of your healing power Jesus. I start this journal praising you and giving you all the glory – for all you are and all you have done and continue to do in me.

Thank you, Lord, from the depths of my being for life and breath – for each day – for today. For miraculously healing the cancer in my body this past year. You have truly worked a wonder. [Last July] I was so sick and there was so much cancer in me and I didn't even know it. A year ago, Aug. 23, 2004, changed my life forever. Dear Lord – please continue your healing. I claim it now – this moment – not just over my body, but my mind and soul. Heal the fears and anxieties – you know them full well. I give myself completely to you. Transform me, oh Lord – deepen my faith and my walk with you. Sharpen my purpose and let me live fully for you.

What a journey this is with my beloved parents – Mum in assisted living – Dad has been in the hospital for 3 weeks and now on to a skilled nursing facility – clinging to life – frail and childlike and yet praising you and telling me to "be strong in the Lord and the power of His might." I will strive to keep that legacy – his legacy of faith and pass it on to my children.

Dryw is on the road with his band. Teach him, Lord, and please protect him. Shape him into a man after your own heart

– use his talents and gifts for your glory. Keep him safe, Lord. May he be rooted and grounded in you with stability and direction in his life.

Thank you for the joy of my Daniel. Please bless him and teach him about you thru me. Help me to be a better mum to him and to bring strong wonderful memories that will sustain him and last his lifetime. Please Lord, give me life to see him grown and settled. I pray that you will give Bill and I life so that our Daniel will not have to experience the loss of either (or both) parents at a young age.

For my Bill – please encourage and strengthen him. Give him a closer walk with you and a hunger to spend time in your word and in prayer. Deepen his faith. Help me be a supportive and loving wife to him.

Father I thank you for the blessings of my friends – all they mean to me – Thank you especially for Barbara D. Her kindness and generosity in making this time possible – this moment of tranquility – a true gift. May she come to know you as her savior. I give this home to you. Fill it with your presence.

I give my family – each precious one to your care, Lord.

Please keep my body strong and healthy. I love you, Lord, with all my heart.

***

Shalita's dad struggled with pneumonia, complicated with an existing heart condition, and had been in and out of the hospital since early February. Shalita was so worried about her dad, but of course there was little that we could do. As her dad declined, she felt the unnatural reversal of roles as the tower of strength and support he had always been slowly gave way to a child-like dependency. Shalita put her thoughts into a poem.

August 2, 2005
Circle of Life

I am becoming a mother to my dad
He whose strong shoulders once carried me to bed
Whose breadth on whom I could once lay my head
Now I wrap those same shoulders close in my arms
And lay that precious head close to mine
Dad's arms gave me shelter and love that was strong
A safe haven to hide even when I did wrong
Now my own arms cradle the one who first cradled me
When to this life I was born.

Circle of life – how fleeting is your passage
The child – now a woman and the man my sweet father
Now rests in my arms like my own little son
Time passes on and yet has just begun
A step closer each day to the race that is won
In this journey of life that will soon take us home
To the arms of our Lord from which no one can roam
I soothe his sweet face and imprint it to mind
For I know that someday I will need to remind
That my dad, so precious will one day be me
When in time I become, a daughter to my son.

By early September, Dad had had enough of hospitals and nursing homes and was ready to let go. It was decided he would leave the hospital and begin hospice at home. In a few days he was gone. Everyone in the family loved Dad, and the loss to Shalita in particular was devastating.

September 8, 2005
Today my dear sweet, precious, beloved Dad – my own Binki slipped out of this world into the arms of Jesus – a warrior

won the battle and celebrates his resurrection day today. The world is poorer, yet heaven rejoices – the angels sing as the gates are flying wide open to receive a true and devoted servant of God. There is a hole in my heart – painful and empty and the tears cannot stop. No one will ever love me like my Dad – his steadfast belief in me – his unconditional love. He showed me to live a life of courage and integrity. To stand for what is right and true – even if it meant standing alone. To never lead a life compromised in purpose. Dad and I are more alike than I realize. This past week Dad said, "Don't hang on to me but never forget me. Be strong in the Lord and in the power of His might." Jesus – you blessed me in my Dad so abundantly. I will carry on his legacy of service and devotion to you and my family.

A Clean Grief

No words left unspoken
No hurts not yet healed
No guilt – no regret of the way things might have been
Clear this valley of grief into which I now walk
Full of rocks and hard places yet uncluttered by fear
Sweet memories sustain me that I now hold so dear
The loss that I feel lies so deep in my heart
Yet I know that in Jesus, Dad will never be apart
I now must live on – each day to its fullest
Knowing his legacy within me still lives on in my soul
So while tears freely flow and I grieve for my dad
I feel no regret – of this I am glad
For I loved him to my fullest
Said to him all that I did
Knew that he knew and nothing was hid
To the end he was my hero and forever will be
His courage undaunted his faith never waivered
Trusted Jesus to take him back home to His glory
And his life now in heaven tells of a brand new story
How I need that deep faith to comfort me now
As I face a new day though I do not know how

Yet this I do know that I stand not alone
For the love sweet Dad gave me will live on in my soul.

Shalita's dad was deeply devoted to his faith and to his family. He was easy to love and, like most that knew him, I always looked up to him. As the youngest, Shalita was daddy's girl. They enjoyed a very special relationship.

September 24, 2005, Stanford
Dad's homecoming feels so unreal – The void in my life feels painful and empty. Grief hits me in waves. I miss him so much, yet I rejoice and feel Dad rejoicing in heaven, peaceful, no pain, no illness – a whole new heavenly body. I think so much about eternity – what is Dad doing? What is his soul experiencing? The body is truly a shell. Thank you, Lord, for being my salvation and that death is only a temporary separation and that someday we will all be reunited and it will be glorious.

September 27, 2005
A clear CT scan – CA 125 of 3.

Dad is my special angel in heaven pleading and interceding at the very throne of God for my total and complete healing. Daddy, I miss you so much. I look at your picture and want to jump inside and feel your arms around me and see your sweet face. I know you are in me and the pain of losing you physically is a deep pain and I ache to my core. It is a clean grief – unclouded by words left unsaid or love not expressed. You know how deeply I loved you and always will.

Dear Lord, My heavenly Father, now you have my earthly father in your arms – what a wonderful reflection he was to me of you and your love. Thank you Father for giving him to me for these 46 years of my life.

December 27, 2005

Thank you Lord for life and breath – for eternity and your infinite purpose for me – for firmly pulling me back to my center in you. For reminding me how fleeting my time on earth is and how much I need to lean on you and trust. Forgive me Lord for shifting my focus to things other than you. The sin around and within me is as insidious as cancer. It creeps in and proliferates without warning. Keep me ever vigilant Lord – ever humble and ever devoted to you. Please deepen and strengthen my prayer life. Lead me to a daily discipline of spending time in you for you are my Only Hope – my Peace. You have led me through so much and carried me each step of the way. I love you Lord – I need you Father. Change my heart, oh God – fan the flame in me. Give me a clearer vision – a purpose for my days on this earth. You have spared my life for a purpose – given me a second chance to live – let me not waste a moment being seduced by worldly desires.

Father please clear my mind and focus my heart. As the psalmist prayed: 'Unite my heart to fear thy name' give me an unburdened heart oh God!

What am I leaving behind? Make my life count Lord – as a disciple of yours – as a wife, mother, daughter, sister, friend, aunt, teacher – I worship you.

Thank you for a good appointment with Dr. Scudder. Unlikely recurrence of my cancer – waiting for a PET scan – trusting you all the way. You are Bigger, Lord – I love you.

Amen

Chapter 10

Remission

After Shalita's recovery from chemo we had a new perspective, one that can only come from being forced to the edge of life and looking into the great abyss. Although we were better at talking about things we wanted to do rather than making them happen, we did follow through on a plan to take a cruise with our boys.

We had originally booked a cruise in the fall of 2004 with Shalita's parents, however, because she was undergoing chemotherapy, we were forced to cancel the trip. In early February 2006 I began looking at cruises, and we settled on one along the Mexican Riviera with Carnival Cruise line. We booked it at the last minute. After years of talking and dreaming about it, were excited to finally go on our first cruise together.

We drove down to Long Beach, boarded the ship, and set sail south toward Puerto Vallarta. It didn't take long for all of us to fall in love with the many indulgences of a cruise. Shalita and I found it to be fun and very relaxing. From her journal:

> **March 4, 2006**
> Somewhere in the Pacific Ocean off the coast of Baja – having afternoon tea in the Raphael Room of the Carnival Pride cruise ship – listening to a chamber orchestra play Bach's Brandenburg Concerto No. 4. Watching the waves go by an endless expanse of ocean – the willing sound of the ocean soothing and healing my soul.
>
> This past week has been a dream – a last minute dream come true that came together despite all odds – A 7 day cruise to the Mexican Riviera – stopping at Puerto Vallarta, Mazatlan and Cabo San Lucas. Memories etched in my heart for a lifetime. A beautiful ocean view, top deck balcony cabin – waking up to the waves and being lulled to sleep by the ocean.

Breathtaking sunsets over the balcony – gazing at the stars and moon sending countless diamonds on the black sea at night. Being reminded of the vastness of God's love for me – *Wide, wide as the ocean, deep, deep as the deepest sea is my Savior's love.*

Delicious meals prepared for me – beds turned down at night (with chocolate!), made for me in the morning. No laundry, dishes – anything. What a gift. Thank you, Lord – Tomorrow it's back to reality. ☺ I praise you, Lord, for this time.

We all enjoyed the cruise and found it both relaxing and fun to be together as a family. From notes I wrote on the trip:

March 4, 2006
I feel completely at peace at this moment. To my right, three large, sturdy windows. Through these windowpanes the vast Pacific Ocean spans east to the horizon. While not visible, Baja and its sandy beaches lie quietly calling. Behind me a violin and piano duet entertain the small chattering crowd that has gathered for tea. Across the small, round wooden table sits my wife. She too writes, opines and tears up as she thinks of returning home and missing terribly the luxury (endless plates of) food and smiles of this cruise – our maiden voyage. The mixture of sounds, sights and rumbling engine make an ideal blend for the senses. What fun!

***

A New Mission

In early 2006 Shalita began developing and giving talks using her own recent experiences of undergoing a devastating diagnosis, surgery, and treatment, combined with her years of experience as a professor of human development. The focus of the talks was the effect of catastrophic illness on the family. She found that it was an area often overlooked, and she was a natural at combining the coursework she had developed for her classes with her own personal diagnosis and treatment, as well as noting the effects of her illness on each one of us.

In her notebook was the word *THRIVER*, an acronym she constructed:

*T*ested and Thankful – each day for life, hair, food!
*H*ealing vs. curing – journey vs. destination. We are in process
*R*enewed every day – new hope (for a cure) mental, spiritual, refocus and reframe
*I*ntrospective – looking inside. Letting go of past hurts. Living purposefully and with deliberation.
*V*igilant – of our health – physical and mental. In tune with our bodies.
*E*mpathetic – never lose touch with pain. Unique kinship we share.
*R*eady to move forward! With hope and celebration. "My life is better now." Measuring life by depth not by its length. Making each day count.

Then she wrote: "When the curtain comes down, you begin Act II. You begin to *live* with purpose and meaning." While initially hesitant to speak in front of groups because of lingering "chemo brain," she managed to not only pull together a logical and coherent presentation, but the several presentations she gave were very well received.

One of the presentations was to the Northern California Home Economics Association, a group she had been a part of when she was a professor at Sierra College. Another talk was to a group of registered nurses at UC Davis Medical Center. She had hit on a vital topic—the effect of catastrophic illness on the family—that was not well understood or discussed in or out of the medical community. The feedback she received was overwhelmingly positive.

May 4, 2006

I am 47 years old today. Happy birthday to <u>me</u> – God's own child, saved and redeemed and healed by my beloved Lord. Parents' only daughter, only sister to my dear brothers, loving wife to my precious husband Bill, mother to my sweet sons, sister-in-law, aunt, friend and <u>CANCER SURVIVOR</u>. All this only thru the grace of my Lord and Savior Jesus Christ.

Thank you Lord for each day – each moment of each year of my life. Even the tough times You have been so faithful and true – always holding me. I am deeply grateful to you, Father, for all your blessings to me. For saving my life and healing me, my Yahweh Rophe [The Lord who heals]. For my beloved family and friends – the promise and beginning of a new ministry. Lord I love you. Thank you. You know the future and are already in it. Sanctify each day Lord. I commit my life to you. You know the deepest prayer of my heart – life, to see Dryw settled, my Daniel an adult and years together with my Bill.

Most of all, Father, I want your purpose fulfilled in me. I give you each day of this year and every year. Fill it and me with joy and peace. I miss my sweet Daddy so much but I know he is here with me and his love lives on in me.

Please give my sweet Mum good health and long life. Father I adore you and worship you with every breath I take. Thank you for my life.

***

In the spring of 2006, we became concerned when a blood test showed Shalita's CA 125 level had risen, if only modestly. The test results were well within the "normal" range, but it concerned us. It was the first sign of a potential problem and each of us, I think, refused to allow ourselves to think that it was anything more than a blip in the test, an anomaly.

122

June 6, 2006

. . . Thank you Father – my sweet precious Jesus, my savior and Lord and Holy Spirit, my comfort, Guide and Peace. I give to you all the days and moments of my life – Make my life an offering of blessing and peace to you. I worship you and stand amazed at your glory.

Father God, I know that you are life and I claim your life and breath in me. I have been reminded yet again how stealthily and insidiously fear of recurrence can creep up on me. My CA 125 went from 5 to 12 – still normal but elevated. Father God – you healed me and brought me thus far. I pray with all my heart that I may not have a recurrence of cancer. Please spare my life for my family – Bill and the boys need me so much – my Mum, brothers, friends, sisters too. My work is not done, Lord. I want so much to live and proclaim your power. I feel you opening up a ministry for me. Please Lord, pour the sweet healing oil of your Holy Spirit on me – let it bathe every cell and organ in my body – renewing, healing and restoring me. I know you are doing this, Father. Please give me a sign of a lowered CA 125 at my next blood test – not a further elevation. Fill me with your healing and peace my El Rophe [Most high God]. You are to be praised.

Please help me to walk the path ahead with courage – Only you, Jesus – only you – be my guide and my light. Shine your light on me, oh Father, please.

Chapter 11

The Ceiling Comes Down Again

On June 18, 2006, Shalita and I celebrated our twelfth wedding anniversary in Santa Rosa. Less than an hour from the ocean and nestled in the heart of Sonoma County's wine country, it had become one of our favorite destinations over the years. We shopped and walked around the quaint downtown area. The next day, a Monday, we had nothing planned, but were simply enjoying the area before heading back to Sacramento. It was a typical, clear, sunny afternoon, and as we drove through nearby Sebastopol, a spa caught my eye. I suggested we get a massage and Shalita agreed. While I had a massage, Shalita opted for a mineral bath. When we were finished, we found a diner across the street and decided to have a late lunch there.

The restaurant was simple, but fit the bill for a quick, light meal. We ordered a couple of sandwiches. About halfway through lunch, Shalita spilled her glass of water. Embarrassed, she asked the waitress for a towel to dry the table and floor. Our waitress quickly mopped up the mess and gave her a new glass of water. Not five minutes later I watched Shalita set her glass of water down again, and as she did, the bottom of her glass hit the edge of her plate, and once again, water spilled over the table and onto the floor. I laughed at her. "I can't believe you did that again!" I blurted out. Now thoroughly embarrassed, she apologized repeatedly to our waitress as she mopped up the spill.

I continued to chuckle about her mishap and remember teasing her later that day when we got home. We attributed her clumsiness to being so relaxed from the mineral bath. That was the only explanation I could think of as to why she had spilled two glasses of water. We arrived in Sacramento, picked up Daniel at her parents' house, and headed back home. It was a quiet evening after a full weekend and we all went to bed focusing on school and work the next day.

In the morning, as I left for work, I quickly kissed Shalita goodbye. She said she had had a terrible night. I said I was sorry, but didn't think much of it. I grabbed a quick breakfast before heading out the door. At the time I was a supervisor at the Energy Commission, and was usually very busy throughout the day with meetings, answering questions from my staff, and responding to an inordinate amount of email. Around 2:30 that afternoon, I slipped out of a meeting to grab something off of my desk when the phone rang. I paused for a moment and debated on whether or not to take the call. I decided to answer.

It was Shalita. I was used to getting calls from her, but this one was different. She said she was in the Costco parking lot and something was wrong with her. She said she was having trouble walking and that her right hand was bothering her. She sounded scared.

All I could think of was it sounded like a stroke, but that seemed so unlikely. Worried, I told her to call 911. As we hung up, I was troubled, but mostly puzzled. I quickly told my boss what had happened and his response was simply, "Go!" On the way home she called and said she was going to the hospital. By the time I caught a light-rail train to my car and then drove to the hospital, an hour had passed.

Shalita was at the ER at Sutter General Hospital in downtown Sacramento. When I got to the ER, I checked in with the woman at the counter and was told that Shalita was seeing one of the doctors. She instructed me to take a seat. After several minutes I approached the window again, but this time no one was there. I waited several minutes until a different woman showed up and asked what I wanted. I explained that I wanted to see my wife. She said they were short staffed and to take a seat. Frustrated, I looked at my watch and noticed a half an hour had elapsed since I had arrived at the ER. After some terse words with the nurse, they finally let me back to see her. I was relieved. She looked concerned and tired, but otherwise appeared okay.

She explained that after she spoke with me on the phone, she drove home, ignoring my suggestion of calling 911, and struggled to use her right hand and foot. When she arrived home she had Dryw take her to see her primary care physician, Dr. Kay Judge, who was located just across the street from the hospital. When Dr. Judge heard Shalita's symptoms, she became very concerned and immediately put her in a wheelchair and personally pushed her across the street to the ER. There Dr. Judge expressed the seriousness of Shalita's symptoms, allowing her to get checked in and seen immediately by a physician.

After a quick examination, the attending physician, Dr. John Fischer, sent her to have a CT scan. As Shalita and I waited for Dr. Fischer to return, I chatted with her and tried to lighten the mood. We were hoping that the diagnosis would be uncomplicated and she would be quickly released. Our friendly banter stopped as Dr. Fischer approached.

A serious looking man in his late fifties, he briefly introduced himself. "We got the results from the CT scan." Without a pause or the slightest hint of concern in his emotionless face, he blurted out words we were not prepared to hear: "They found two masses in the brain, which are likely tumors." *Did he say tumors? He said tumors. Two brain tumors.*

As I turned to Shalita, our eyes locked. Instantly I saw her ebony eyes well up with tears. For that moment, time stopped. As the thoughts floated in mid-air inside our heads we struggled to process the devastating words we had just heard.

"I'm sorry, I'm so sorry," Shalita said to me.

"Don't say that," I said.

"I am sorry you have to go through this," she continued.

"Shalita, you have nothing to be sorry about," I said as tears began to stream down my face. For the second time, the roof had collapsed on top of us and we were crushed by the weight of the news.

As Dr. Fischer disappeared from view, a nurse approached. She had seen the frightened look on our faces. "You seem like a nice family and I wanted to know if there was anything I could do." As I struggled to regain my composure I told her that I was going outside to call family and asked her if she could make sure I could get back in without having to wait another thirty minutes. She assured me that she would make sure I could get back in without a problem.

The next few moments are a blur, but as the implications of the initial diagnosis began to sink in, I distinctly remember a strange thought: *I never bought a Mustang.* It was as if this iconic car symbolized the many things that Shalita and I had talked about doing, but hadn't. Of course it wasn't about a car; it was the regret of all the things we had dreamed about, places we would visit together, things we wanted to do. It was unfinished business, a long checklist of things that we had created, but sometime after our mouths gave birth to the dreams, they died somewhere along the way. *Would we ever go back to Paris? Would we see Austria or take Daniel to India? Would we ever drive up the Pacific Coast Highway in an open convertible—a Mustang convertible?*

Still in a state of shock, Shalita was given steroids to reduce the swelling in her head, which was affecting the motor skills on the right side of her body. I went outside the ER to deliver the news to my brother-in-law John. I struggled to find the right words. Next I called Deb. I hated being the one to deliver this horrible blow, but I had bigger things to worry about, I told myself, and there was a part of me that needed to get some of the terrible news off my chest. I could only imagine the impact of the news would have on our families.

Scared and depleted, I left the hospital to pick up Daniel at church. He was there for Summerfest, a three-day extravaganza for kids that is our church's version of Vacation Bible School. I picked him up from inside the church and we walked together to the car. My mind still swirling with the news, I struggled with how and when to tell him. I asked how his day was but my mind was light-years away. I decided to tell him when we got to the car. Daniel was nine at the time. I picked him up and set him on the trunk of my white Toyota Camry. He looked at me, wondering what I was about to tell him. I fumbled through the story explaining what was happening to his mom and the seriousness of the situation the best I could. I remember looking into his eyes and seeing the wheels inside his head turning. I wondered if he understood the gravity of the news I had just delivered. We got in the car and made our way back home, seeking a measure of peace that was now achingly absent.

***

The fears we had in May when Shalita's CA 125 level was elevated turned out to be a harbinger of worse news to come. *Certainly this is an anomaly,* we thought at the time. *It will be lower next time,* we said to each other and prayed that it would be so. And while the level of this tumor marker was nowhere near 9,800, as it was when she was originally diagnosed, the elevated level indeed signaled a recurrence of cancer.

The next day the medical staff discussed the possibility of treating the tumors with a gamma knife, an elaborate and expensive piece of equipment that uses gamma radiation to precisely target and kill the cancer cells that make up a tumor. And while Sutter did not have a gamma knife, UC Davis Medical Center, just a few miles away, did have one.

Shalita was still at Sutter General when one of the women in our cancer support group came to visit. Like many in the group, she was a breast cancer survivor. She was grim. I could tell she was deeply troubled to see Shalita this way. She was probably thinking, *This could be me*. When she left Shalita was feeling down and the thoughts of the future weighed on us both. Not long after, another woman from the cancer support group paid a visit. She had called me first and asked if there was anything she could do. I told her that Shalita was discouraged and that the best thing would be to see if she could cheer her up. Vicki Becker, the wonderful ex-Brit, came with a sharp sense of humor. Her visit brought the sunshine back to an otherwise dark and cloudy day. It was amazing that, in just a few minutes, Vicki brought us both back up and provided some perspective that was desperately needed. I don't recall Vicki's exact words but she basically said not to be too concerned, this was just a "bump in the road." As it turned out, it was a hell of a bump, but it was a relief to think about this recurrence as just a part of our new-normal life, rather than the beginning of the end.

Shalita was soon transferred to UC Davis Medical Center. We were told that Shalita's tumors were too large for her to be a good candidate for the gamma knife. Instead, she would require two conventional brain surgeries to remove the tumors. Dr. Chang, her new doctor, evaluated Shalita and walked us through the procedures, the risks and recovery. On the day of the first surgery, June 22, we both felt anxious about the procedure, knowing that, unlike her abdominal surgery to remove cancer around her ovaries, this would be trickier. They would be removing a portion of her skull and delicately removing the tumor that was attached to the brain. We were told that the surgery could cause temporary or permanent damage to key regions of the brain, and that the partial paralysis on her right side could be permanent.

As the time for the surgery approached, two men came in to put her on a gurney and wheel her to pre-op. "Can you give us 5 minutes?" I asked. "Sure," one of them responded and the men disappeared. The uncertainty that lay ahead felt overwhelming. I climbed up onto her narrow hospital bed and we held each other. For a few precious moments, we were able to block out the present frightening world around us. In those brief heartbeats, we laid our petition before God. We held each other tightly and did our best to fight the fears we each felt.

Deana arrived just as the staff returned to transfer Shalita on to the gurney. Holding Shalita's hand, I looked into her beautiful eyes. They were clear and focused. When we arrived at pre-op we said our goodbyes and all three of us put up a confident facade. As they pushed the gurney through the tall metal doors, we held our breath.

Deana and I left and turned the corner, and as we did, the proverbial dam broke. We both burst into tears. We hugged and told each other that she was in God's care now. As our composure slowly returned, we made our way to the waiting room, greeted by family and friends that had come to support us and pray and hope for the best outcome.

We had been directed by the medical staff to go to the public area near the entrance rather than the surgery waiting room. Unlike most of the typically whitewashed, sterile hospital, the entrance was all brick. The dark burgundy color gave the area a somewhat classy look. As I milled about the area, catching up with friends and trying desperately not to think too much about the surgery, the waiting dragged on. When Dr. Chang came out, he asked to speak with me. A small group of us huddled together, waiting intently to hear the news of how the surgery went.

We were greatly relieved to hear that it went well and tried hard to follow his explanation of the procedure and Shalita's condition. Each sentence was carefully constructed so that any prognosis was measured. "She will have temporary paralysis of her right side. It's possible that it could be permanent," he said. While almost any news that there were no complications from the surgery were welcome, those words "paralysis" and "could be permanent" replayed in my mind over and over that day.

Before long Shalita was transferred to post-op, and I was told it would be a few hours still until I could see her. She was quite a sight—connected to tubes, head wrapped in gauze. Like her recovery after her surgery in August 2004, I was overcome with the flood of feelings seeing her this way. Her first words were: "Hi, honey. So did they go inside my head?" "Yes they did," I responded. "Wow," she replied. And I realized what a strange thing to think about—that this amazingly complex brain of ours that allows us to talk, move, do almost anything with our bodies, was thinking about just being operated on. Her recovery went well, and in a few days we were talking about the second surgery to remove the other tumor. Having been through the first surgery, we were all less afraid this time. Shalita was very confident that God would get her through this one too.

Seven days after her first, she underwent her second brain surgery. Again, we anxiously waited downstairs near the main entrance of Medical Center. And again, Dr. Chang came out and met with us to discuss the procedure. She had made it successfully through this one as well. I felt a tremendous sense of relief. This recovery, however, was more painful and difficult for her. Where she had bounced back quite quickly the week earlier, this one took more time.

On the Fourth of July, Shalita was still in the hospital recovering. For many years our family tradition on the Fourth was getting together with our good friends the Robertsons. That summer, however, things were very different and we began looking at options of how to include Shalita in the celebration. After some thought, I talked with the nurses and asked if we could take her home. The nurses said no, she wasn't ready to leave the hospital. Crushed, I decided to talk with another nurse. After a lengthy talk and much pleading, we were allowed to "unofficially" take Shalita home for a few hours to celebrate the holiday, if I promised to bring her back by ten p.m. It was a deal I gladly took. Kim Robertson and I planned it out, calling it "the great escape." With bandages wrapped around her head and in a wheelchair, Shalita was able to be with us for dinner and fireworks. It became the most memorable Fourth of July celebration we all had together.

* * *

The summer of 2006 was a particularly crazy time for the Blackburns. After Shalita was released from the hospital, we had several members of her family stay with us at our home. Everyone wanted to help us out and, of course, spend time with Shalita.

Shalita's mom stayed with us for a week and a half. She was a big comfort to Shalita and a tremendous help. After her mom left, Shalita's cousin Averil from Washington DC came out and stayed with us. Shalita very much enjoyed catching up with Averil. Next, Shalita got a call from another cousin, Charlene, from Maryland. She asked if she could come and help. Her husband, Terry, also asked if he could come, but only if he could be of help. Terry had recently retired as a mathematician from the federal government.

We both felt it was a very thoughtful offer. Shalita, never being one to say no to help, told him to come and remodel our spare half bathroom. It seemed odd at the time to ask such a request since it had little to do with helping Shalita, or me for that matter. But Shalita saw a generous offer and gladly accepted. When I think of it now, I still laugh at the thought of Terry traveling three thousand miles to remodel our little half bath in the family room.

As Shalita and Charlene visited and caught up, Terry inquired as to what we wanted to do for the bathroom. I showed him how the base of the toilet was loose and that simply tightening the bolts holding its foundation did nothing to make it more secure. The wood floor under the toilet seemed to be rotted. I explained to Terry what we were thinking to fix up the bathroom and told him how to get to our neighborhood Home Depot to get him started. Terry was a man on a mission. If Shalita said the bathroom needed a good remodel, he was going to do it in the week they were with us.

It was a very difficult week, as Shalita was still frail and moved around the house slowly, limping back and forth between the family room and the kitchen. To compound things, we experienced one of the worst heat waves in decades. Several records were set—twelve days in a row of daily highs above 100 degrees. It was so bad that hundreds died in California, including more than a dozen in Sacramento. The delta breeze that usually blows east from the San Francisco Bay, something Sacramentans count on in the summer, didn't come. The heat was so intense and continuous that our house air conditioner was on all the time, yet it couldn't cool the house below 82 degrees. On top of the heat, Shalita was running a fever. Chris had warned us to watch out for fevers, explaining that infections could be deadly.

The heat and the constant worry of Shalita's fever stressed me out. To add to my concern, the sealant that Terry was using on the damaged wood in the bathroom floor smelled up the entire house. Worried about Shalita's fever, not being able to cool the house down, and now the smell of toxic sealant permeating the house, I finally sent Shalita to a friend's house to stay for a few nights while Terry finished up. I wasn't much help, but to Terry's credit, he worked like a madman to finish up the remodel and did a fantastic job. And after a few days away, Shalita came home well rested and happy to be with her family.

Chapter 12

Coping with Catastrophic Illness

Shalita's recovery from her second brain surgery was slow and difficult. But the challenges of recovery were tempered by an overwhelming amount of love and support we felt from family and friends. In addition to the family help, we had meals regularly brought to us from many friends and acquaintances, particularly from our church. That made my job a little easier during Shalita's slow recovery. While she improved a little each week, she never fully regained the motor skills in both her right arm and right leg. She needed assistance doing many simple daily activities and walking was more difficult. I realized that after the surgeries our roles had somewhat reversed, as I made sure she and the boys were properly fed, did laundry, and took her to seemingly endless medical appointments. A new reality for me, I found my role as caregiver very difficult at times.

These added responsibilities were on top of my full-time job as a supervisor overseeing a popular and often hectic solar rebate program at the state's Energy Commission. I began to see that trying to fulfill my roles as both supervisor and part-time caregiver at home simply wasn't going to work. My management was extremely supportive, and I was fortunate to be able to reduce my work hours to fifty percent, although I often worked more than that to keep up with my responsibilities.

At home, one of the things that was hardest for me was that Shalita sometimes moaned when she wasn't feeling well. While it often wasn't intense pain she was experiencing, it was just her body's way of dealing with the discomfort. But the moans got to me, not unlike a child banging on a tin can. It seemed to go on and on. I found myself getting irritable and impatient. I knew I needed some time to myself or to get out with a friend, but it was hard to make that happen. And, of course, I wanted to spend as much time with Shalita as I could.

***

August 2006

One day, while driving home, I noticed a beautiful sunset in the western sky. It was nothing spectacular, but it was a lovely mix of oranges, yellows, and grays. When I got home, I told Shalita I wanted to show her something and whisked her to the car. We drove one block from our home and I showed her the sunset. She admired it and smiled. We sat there for ten or fifteen minutes, holding hands, grateful to God for simple beauties.

Late that summer Shalita received a letter from her childhood friend, Chutku. She had heard of Shalita's recurrence and subsequent surgeries. On the top of the letter was a lipstick impression of lips that read underneath: "Two kisses superimposed!"

New Delhi
25th July 2006

My Darling Shalita,
You are always in my thoughts, prayers and heart. As I write this letter to you I can remember so clearly the ones we wrote to each other when we were children. We were and are truly blessed to have each other. I cannot even imagine my childhood without you in it; as important as my family. It hurts when I go to Allahabad and don't find you there. But, we have much to be grateful for. For all the years we had together.

I pray that you have made a complete recovery and that the Lord takes you from strength to strength each day. When He finds a way for me to visit you we will have to forgo sleep and chat through the night (with maybe a midnight feast thrown in!). We know that He heals and soon your illness will be completely behind you. I have faith that the Lord will touch and heal you.

My darling friend, how I ache to put my arms around you and tell you how much you mean to me.

Today is a lovely rain-washed day here. What a relief from the oppressive heat! Some years back I realized that our beautiful gardens didn't just happen on their own and I began a bit of hands-on gardening. Today, after the rain it's looking washed and rather pretty so I walked out and plucked a flower for you – with all my love, sweetheart!

Ishan (nearly 17) and Jainvi (14 ½) have their 12th and 10th board exams in March and I (a glutton for punishment) have got myself an Irish Setter pup, Leo, who gives me the run around all day. Ishan and Jainvi want to train him to carry a brick in his mouth like Brutus!

The T.V. Raos plan to be in Delhi en masse next week. Sarita's [Chutku's sister] older son is visiting from Canada. The younger one is in England. Rajesh [Chutku's brother-in-law] divides his time between Delhi and London and has taken a house on rent there. We could consider meeting up there next summer. I do hope we can work something out – it's been too long to be away from loved ones.

Before I end I want you to tell Aunty, Chris and John that I love them and miss them so much. I will be writing again soon.

My very special love, hugs and kisses to Bill, Dryw and Daniel. My biggest, tightest hug and lots of kisses to you. Take care, God Bless.

Love you,
XXXXXXX Chutku

***

During the fall of 2005, before her recurrence, Shalita and I had traveled to Las Vegas, along with Chris, Deb, John and Deana. It was the first time the six of us had taken a vacation together and we had a great time. During the summer of 2006 we began talking about all six of us traveling together again in the fall. This time, however, Shalita's surgeries and radiation treatment had taken a heavy toll on her, and we knew that she didn't have the strength to do anything too ambitious and, I believe, each of us knew that this might be the last time we would be able to do something like this together because of the uncertainty of her health.

We decided on going to San Antonio, Texas, in mid-November. We booked three nights at the Marriott hotel along the city's beautiful River Walk. While Shalita could walk, her movements were slow and labored. She tilted slightly to the side and, despite months of physical therapy at the UC Davis Medical Center; she still lacked full use of her motor skills on the right side.

Shortly before we departed for San Antonio, Shalita had noticed a lump on her neck and had it biopsied, and of course we both were concerned that it was a new tumor. While we didn't know for sure if it was malignant or benign, we were all worried. The future felt like a series of large dark clouds on the horizon that, again, were heading our way. It cast a pall over our time in San Antonio, feelings that seemed impossible to escape.

While in Texas, we saw the sights in San Antonio, traveled to Austin, where Chris and Deb had lived during his residency, and enjoyed barbeque at the Salt Lick, a down-home style joint that has become a Texas institution, serving the best slow-smoked ribs I have ever eaten. The last evening in San Antonio, we wandered along the River Walk and stopped at a restaurant where a small jazz band played outdoors not far from the river. We sat and listened to the smooth saxophone and drums. We requested they play "Take Five" by the Dave Brubeck Group. The sweet sounds resonated with Shalita and me, and for a few joyous moments our minds were carried off to a place far away, removed from the hard realities of present and future.

***

Because her right hand and arm were impaired from the surgeries, Shalita essentially stopped writing. Her handwriting had always been beautiful. Now it was a struggle to write anything legible.

The last page of her journal was not a typical entry—how could it be? The elegant handwriting she used was now little more than a scribble. The words were few, but telling.

2006 – June 20 – Sutter ER
June 22 – 1st surgery for brain tumor UCDMC
June 29 – 2nd surgery
July 27 – Started radiation

The combination of her two brain surgeries and her radiation treatment left her hair very short, with major scars that remained as evidence of the operations. When Shalita lost her hair in 2004 due to her chemo treatments she found a wig to wear. After her more recent hair loss she again went shopping for a wig, and she was a good sport about it. During a visit to Wigs R You in October 2006, a reporter from *The Sacramento Bee* interviewed her. The story was published on December 8, 2006. It was one of her last times Shalita went into a store. The article was called "Making Bald Beautiful," and told the story of this small shop catering to women going through cancer treatment. An excerpt from the article:

"Oh, we do get stories," [owner Cindy] Jacobs says, her eyes welling with tears for the third time today. "They weigh on me."

Every day she scans the obituaries, hoping against hope that none of her former clients is listed.

Jacobs and the others have happy stories, too. Stories of clients who come into the shop hanging their heads, and leave with their eyes twinkling. Celebrations, complete with sparkling cider, of the end of treatments and the beginning of new lives. Laughter when a wig transforms a timid dishwater blonde into the bold redhead she's always wanted to be.

"I'm 73 years old and I've done a lot of things, and it's like God saved the best for last for me," says staffer Eileen Vance, standing in the back room of the shop on a November

afternoon, styling refurbished wigs that clients can borrow if they cannot afford the $195 to $300 cost of a new one.

"Every day I wonder, 'What kind of angel is going to walk in here today?' These women give us the most wonderful gifts."

Long-term relationships

Shalita Blackburn is one of those angels. On a quiet weekday morning, Blackburn, a willowy former college professor, strolls up to the counter. She sniffs the scent of lavender, hears the soft music, spots familiar faces.

Greeting Tron [a worker], she matter-of-factly pulls off her auburn wig for a fluff and a style.

It has been two years, Blackburn recalls, since she first set foot in the store, shortly after being diagnosed with ovarian cancer. She found a hairpiece and new friends. She fought the cancer and got her hair back. Now she is thin and bald and weak again, fighting a recurrence that has spread to her brain.

Hair loss may seem like the least of her troubles, Blackburn says.

"But it's a physical reminder of your illness. The first time you lose it, it's horrifying. So many women define themselves by their physical beauty, and your hair is such a big part of that, even though in reality it's a small part of who we are."

Blackburn looks around the wig shop, with its muted lighting and comfortable sofa and inspiring words on the walls. Here, she says, she feels safe and nurtured.

"What they do here," she says, "is so much more than fitting a wig. It's a very healing place."

140

With Tron's help, Blackburn maneuvers her wig back into place. She checks her look in the mirror and nods her approval. After Tron wraps her in a tight hug, the angel walks out into the sunshine.[3]

---

[3] *Sacramento Bee,* Article found at:
http://www.wigsryou.com/sacbee_12_06.html

Chapter 13

A Cold Winter

When we returned home from San Antonio, we received news that the lump on her neck was a malignant tumor. We were very disappointed, but not surprised. It was a minor procedure to have it removed.

In late November, Shalita and I were talking in our bedroom. She wanted to make plans for Christmas and the holiday season. Immediately, I felt a sense of dread welling up inside me. Many times before we had clashed over details of how we would spend the holidays and which family we would be with, etc. It was one of my least favorite subjects. I wanted to avoid or at least postpone our talk until it was closer to Christmas.

As I groaned about even discussing the subject, Shalita became annoyed. Frustrated at my reluctance to talk, she threw out a statement that caught me off guard.

"I want to make this holiday special because I don't know if I will be around next Christmas," she said.

It stopped me in my tracks. I briefly looked up at her, seeing the pain she was feeling and the sheer weight of what she just said sank in. Immediately my eyes welled up.

"When you say that, I die a thousand deaths," I said, tears now beginning to flow. The idea of this being her last Christmas pounded me. It brought to the surface my greatest fear. As we both cried, we sensed, in a way we hadn't before, the fear we each felt about the future. I know how I felt, but can only imagine the sadness and terror she was feeling, that cancer—this insidious disease—seemed to be gaining ground.

It was the first time I had heard her talk in such frank terms. It was also the first time she had talked about a date in the future, a date that she might not be with us. I knew she was probably right, but I desperately fought inside to avoid thinking such hopeless thoughts. She then said that she was not afraid of dying, but that she was worried about experiencing a lot of pain as the cancer spread. As I listened, I heard the words, but I couldn't fully fathom all that she was communicating. The thought of losing her at this age just wasn't comprehensible. It was far too painful for me to fully absorb.

By early December, Shalita was beginning to experience back pain. She initially thought it was our mattress. While the mattress was several years old, it was quite firm and seemed to work well for both of us, even with my back trouble. As her back pain continued, we found a new mattress that was the same model as we had once slept on while staying at the Westin Saint Francis Hotel in San Francisco. We had spent the weekend there and fell in love with the bed. The new mattress seemed to be the ideal mix of a soft plush top with a firm foundation. We bought it and it was delivered and set up the next day.

I slept well that first night on the new mattress. When I woke up I remember thinking that my back felt better than with our old mattress. So I was surprised when Shalita said: "We have to take it back; it hurts my back." Disappointed, I said: "Let's give a few days at least to see if you get used to it." But the back pain became worse and I knew from my own experiences how debilitating and frustrating the pain could be.

By mid-December, Shalita was also having trouble keeping food down. After unsuccessfully trying different things to ease her discomfort, including changing her medications, she was getting worse. So on the morning of December 19, 2006, I took her back to the hospital. As we drove into downtown Sacramento, we literally debated whether to go to Sutter General or back to UC Davis Medical Center. Right before the exit we decided on Sutter and we went to the ER.

Before long Shalita had another CT scan and was admitted for observation. Later that day, as I was driving on the freeway, my cell phone rang. "This is Dr. Martin calling, is this Mr. Blackburn?"

A wave of sobriety hit me. "Yes," I replied.

"We have the results of the CT scan. The test shows several tumors along her spinal column."

My mouth dropped. *How could this be? Not again.*

But it made sense; it would explain the back pain she was experiencing. For the third time the roof came down and cancer again roared to the front of my brain. Although it didn't pack the same punch as the previous diagnoses, it still left me devastated, searching for answers.

144

"Let me tell her," I said to the doctor. He agreed. I went home deeply distraught at the news and wondering how I would explain it to her.

At home I collected some things that Shalita would need at the hospital, my head still spinning. We had come so far from June—brain surgeries, radiation treatment, physical therapy. But it was back. *How could this happen again?*

When I returned to the hospital, Shalita was in fairly good spirits. We chatted for a few minutes, I don't remember what about. I decided it was time to tell her. It pained me to just think of it and it pained me even more to have to tell her.

"The doctor called me on the way home. He said the results of the CT scan show that there are tumors along your spinal column."

She looked at me and began to cry. We both cried; crushed and frustrated that this horrible disease was forcing its way back into our lives. I remember those moments of hugs and tears and how incredibly sad I felt. Yet after a few moments, when the tears were gone, there was a strange feeling of lightness. While the news could hardly have been worse, somehow crying had washed away the worst of the sadness that I was feeling. The understanding was there, but the tears had somehow allowed me to grieve for those moments, and then let some of it go, at least briefly.

As I sat on the edge of her hospital bed, propped up at the head, I said something about "when you get home."

"Thank you for saying that I will go home," she said. We hugged. I did my best to reassure her that things were somehow not as bleak as they seemed.

That evening while at home, the reality of Shalita's condition began to sink in. It wasn't long before it became clear that the likelihood of successfully treating several new tumors was not good and my worst fears of losing her began to grow.

The next day Shalita was moved to the oncology section of the hospital. The nursing director on duty that night was Mark, the brother-in-law of a close friend of mine, Lynn. Mark had a round face and a warm smile. As he showed us to the room where Shalita was being admitted, Mark told me that his sister and brother-in-law were struggling with a recent separation. As he discussed the adjustments his brother-in-law was now facing, Mark said, "Change leads to growth." As my distraught mind struggled to focus, I latched on to that phrase—*change leads to growth*—like a toddler clinging to his mother's leg, and I decided then that this would somehow help me make it through the impending storm. I thought, *That's how I'll get through this—the horrible loss of losing Shalita will force me to grow.*

While losing Shalita, I knew, would be more excruciating than anything I had ever faced, I also knew that God would carry me and our two boys through this heartbreaking loss. And through the pain of my world turning upside down, I decided, the resulting growth would provide strength and insight that would help me to continue on with my life. But I was grasping for straws – anything that would ease the immediate and frightening anxiety of what a world without Shalita would be like.

***

The next day I was back at the hospital as they wheeled Shalita on a gurney to radiology. In order to ease her discomfort, she was being sent there to be evaluated for possible radiation treatment to shrink the tumors. Unlike the radiation she had received several months earlier for her brain tumors, this was not intended to cure her, but to minimize the pressure of the tumors on her nerves.

I walked with her as the staff wheeled her across the "tube," a long footbridge that crosses L Street leading from the main hospital to the Sutter Cancer Center. There we met a radiologist who explained the procedure, side effects, etc. He was tall, with a quick grin and a surprisingly chipper demeanor. Wearing a spotless, long white lab coat, he looked part surgeon, part college professor. As he talked eagerly about details of radiation, I noticed he had several pens in his pocket. I counted seven. *Why would he have seven pens in his coat pocket?* I wondered to myself. Suddenly, I was completely distracted by this oddity and found my mind bouncing in and out of his discussion. When he was finished I asked him about the pens. He looked slightly embarrassed. "I inevitably lose pens," he replied. "This way, I usually have one or two by the end of the day." How strange, I thought. Here we were talking about something intensely serious, but somehow my mind focused on this curiously odd habit.

146

Ultimately, radiation therapy was considered impractical because of the number of tumors present and their proximity to the spine. The approach the doctor wanted to take was to insert a device called an ommaya reservoir. This was a specialized catheter used as a delivery device for chemotherapy to be sent into the cerebrospinal fluid in hopes of shrinking the tumors. The procedure involved drilling a small hole in her skull to insert the ommaya. We were told that it was a long shot, but it was the best approach of the limited options. At this point the goal was comfort and extending her life, not curing her.

The procedure to insert the ommaya reservoir went smoothly and chemo was started immediately. A few days after the procedure we celebrated Christmas in her hospital room. A very different Christmas than we had imagined. The ever-present clouds that hung over us grew darker and we suffered through the ups and downs of the doctor's latest updates. We prayed fervently for healing and relief from the increasing amount of pain she was experiencing.

As her pain intensified, I sensed that Shalita's worst fears were coming true—that she would suffer gravely as the cancer advanced. This deeply troubled me, and I asked her physician to bring in a pain specialist, which they promptly did. A course of morphine and other medications were added to her treatment and she was monitored regularly, allowing adjustments to be made based on her level of pain and any side effects. One of the side effects of the cocktail of medicines she was on was that she frequently slipped in and out of consciousness. I felt frustrated. While the medication helped to lessen her level of pain, I could see her still suffering in her sleep or various states of consciousness and communicating with her was now intermittent between states of lucidness and incoherence. It was now rare for her to talk or respond.

One day as I was sitting next to her bed, I was doing my best to talk with her and reassure her in a one-way conversation. Seemingly out of nowhere, she looked intently at me and said loudly, "Why are you doing this to me?"

I was taken aback. "Doing what? What is it babe?" There was no response.

Then again, "Why are you doing this to me?" Her dark brown eyebrows furled; there was anger in her tone. She expressed this again, even more intensely.

"What is it?" I replied. She didn't respond. "I am not doing anything to you, honey. Do you want to stop the treatment? Is that what you're saying? *Is that it?*"

Again, no response. No words, no shaking her head, nothing. As I tried to get her to tell me what it was that was troubling her, she was gone, retreating to a place I could not follow.

As I left the hospital I felt a new burden. Was she trying to tell me she wanted to start hospice and go home to die? Why did she say this to me? Surely she must know in her heart that the last thing I wanted to do was to subject her to more suffering.

I was at a crossroads. A choice had to be made, and no one could make it but me. Should I tell the doctors to continue with treatment in the hopes of extending her life a few weeks or perhaps months, but keep her in the hospital? Or should I tell the doctor that it was time to give up treatment and begin hospice? It was devastating for me to think of giving up any hope of her recovering, even for a short period. But she had been in the hospital now for a month and that was its own torture. Each road seemed bleak. There was no good answer, only certain pain.

As I wrestled inside, searching for an answer, struggling to make sense of her angry outburst, I felt overwhelmed. I called my sister-in-law Deana and we met for coffee that evening at the hospital. As I shared the events of the day, I again found myself crying and explained to her how hard it was to hear what Shalita had said. We talked about the two awful outcomes and the excruciating decision that I had to make. It was one of the lowest times of my life. Talking with Deana helped me unload this burden, if only a little. I will always be grateful to her for helping me through that tortuous time.

From my journal

January 9, 2007
As I sit on this orange couch I hear Michael McDonald sing "All in Love Is Fair"—and I hold the 8 x 10 photo of us four on the cruise – and cry. I hit the button on the remote and hear it again, and again, and again, and again.

Shalita, my lovely, wonderful wife lies in room 4411 and cries in pain. Or perhaps she sleeps, but with a pained look. My heart breaks.

Twenty-two days she has been there. What to do now? More torture, and hope for some additional time of weeks, perhaps months. What an awful choice – each filled with pain. This has been so very hard.

Sometime around early January, several friends had visited Shalita and a few left music CDs. As I played some of the CDs for Shalita, I found them reassuring. In addition to soft classical music, there were a few CDs of contemporary Christian artists. Two songs I remember playing for her resonated with me: Chris Tomlin's "How Great Is Our God" and Michael W. Smith's "Agnus Dei." At the hospital, then later at home, I would play the songs over and over. The songs' repetition was a salve for me, easing some of the pain deep within. It was more powerful than the morphine Shalita was receiving.

Listening to "Agnus Dei," I would close my eyes and sing, "Alleluia, Alleluia, for the Lord God Almighty Reigns." *Holy are you, Lord God Almighty. Worthy is the Lamb.* The soothing melody and repetition carried me away.

***

The decision I had dreaded and agonized over was made. After repeated discussions with Shalita's doctor and brother Chris, on January 19th I decided it was time to stop treatment, bring her home, and begin hospice. The chemotherapy she had received through the ommaya was not working and Shalita's body was failing. She had always been adamant that she did not want to die in a hospital, but at home.

I think she envisioned, as did I, that if and when the day came to be brought home for hospice care, she would be made as comfortable as possible in our bedroom and look out the French doors to our deck and garden. The nurses would check on her regularly, ensuring she had sufficient pain medication. I am sure that she pictured this would be a time that she could visit with family and her many friends—to say goodbye to the many that she loved. It would be a dignified and peaceful end. But Shalita had been in a semi-coma for many days. She had only occasionally spoken during the last three weeks of her life, and now she was weak and continued to receive heavy medication to manage the pain. She would open her eyes at times and I think she could hear much of what we said to her, but she showed little response. The one exception was when Chris told her he was leaving to return home to Milwaukee. With cancer patients of his own, medical students he mentored, and ongoing research, he felt compelled to get back. I know he felt tormented leaving Shalita and the family.

When Chris explained to Shalita that he was going home, she reacted strongly. Although she had shown little responsiveness in more than a week, she cried hearing the news. We were all surprised. Not that she would react to Chris saying goodbye, but that she was able to understand what he told her and that she reacted so dramatically. This, of course, made it even harder for him to leave.

I told Shalita's doctor that we wanted to take her home and start hospice. I was told later in the day that they were unable to transport her home until the following day, Saturday. The explanation for the delay was that with the weekend coming they were short on staff and it took a considerable amount of time and effort to get the medications ready, set up the van to transport her, and provide a portable bed and other medical equipment so that the transition home was as smooth and painless as possible. This made sense to me, and we agreed that she would be brought home the next day. With the help of family, we physically and mentally began the process of preparing the house for her return to home, where she would spend her last days.

When I went back to Sutter on Saturday, Shalita's condition was the same—some alertness but minimal movement and unable to speak. I tried to explain to her the best I knew how that she was going home and that she would be in hospice. While it was a relief that she would be coming home, the central feeling for me was an overwhelming sense of sadness from the stark reality that her life would very soon end.

Instead of bringing her home that Saturday, however, I was again told that it would not work for her to be released—again saying that it was the weekend and the limited staff would not be able to set her up to begin hospice care. I was told she would be released on Monday, January 22. During that time we had the bed and medical equipment delivered, arranged the house to accommodate a hospital bed, and tried to get everything in place the best we could. We began taking down the many cards and notes that friends had written that we had taped to the walls of her hospital room. In talking with Chris, we decided that the best place for her bed would be in our family room. Because of the many friends and family that would come, it seemed the most logical place to set things up.

When Monday came, the plan was she would be released around noon. That morning I received a call from Sutter. I was told that due to staff coming off the weekend, *again* they would be unable to bring her home until the following day. While I had been concerned that she might slip away quickly and die in the hospital, I had been agreeable to the hospital staff's explanation that they could not get her home during the weekend. This time, however, when I got off the phone I was angry. For the third time now it was explained to me that it would be impossible to bring her home that day.

My emotions began to boil and the thoughts racing through my head were pure fury. *This is ridiculous,* I thought. *Don't they realize how important it is that her last breaths not be inside the sterile, bleak confines of a hospital room? She's coming home today!* I picked up the phone and called the nurse I had spoken with a few moments ago. In a firm but calm voice I told the nurse that it was very important that she came home today. "I'm sorry, Mr. Blackburn, but that's *impossible.*"

I said, "Look, it's 10:30 now, so you have several hours before the end of the day to get things together and bring her home. I am not asking you to send someone to the moon, but she needs to come home today!"

"We need Dr. Fischer's signature to release her," she fired back. I was told that Dr. Fischer (my least favorite doctor) was in Marysville, a full hour away. I was having none of it. I explained to her that I would be happy to drive to Marysville and get his signature.

"Listen," I finally said, "Please work with me. We can do this." I don't recall the exact words after that, but she finally realized that I was not backing down. My wife was coming home that day.

"Ok," she finally said, "We will try to release her today." I thanked her and then called Mark, one of the head nurses in the oncology section and the brother-in-law of my good friend Lynn Hutchinson. I explained to Mark what had occurred in the previous three days and asked him to do what he could to help get her home today. He agreed. The many wheels that needed to turn to release a patient began to turn, and at around 5:45 p.m. that evening, Shalita was wheeled on a gurney though our front door. They carefully moved her into the bed that had been set up in our family room. *Thank God she was finally home.*

As the nurses set up their medical equipment and began monitoring her in our modest family room, one of them introduced herself to Shalita. As I watched out of the corner of my eye I witnessed something remarkable. Even though Shalita had shown almost no response for days, she slowly reached her hand up to touch the nurse's face. I couldn't believe it. It was as if she were saying, "Thank you for bringing me home and caring for me." Incredibly weak and heavily medicated, her hand gently stroked the woman's face before she slowly lowered her hand.

***

We welcomed Shalita back home. For the next few days Shalita's family camped out as we took turns spending time with her. We talked with her, held her hand, stroked her hair, sang to her, prayed. We wanted to be there when she would slip away from her troubled world. Chris called shortly after Shalita arrived home and said he was hopping on a plane and would be back the following day. I was surprised but comforted by his decision to return.

Tuesday morning came and we continued to talk and pray with her. The day passed uneventfully. Chris arrived and we were all happy to have him back. That evening I remember thinking that I was exhausted and I had to get some sleep. But it was impossible to really let go and get the rest I needed knowing that she could go at any time. I desperately wanted to be with her the last few hours.

On Wednesday, January 24th, Shalita's breathing became slower and labored. We continued to talk and pray with her. In the afternoon, most of the family went out to pick up some supplies for Shalita's mom. Just Dryw and I were at home with her. By five p.m.

her breathing was visibly slowing. Having witnessed firsthand my mother and father-in-law pass away, I felt certain she was near the end. I phoned Chris and told them to come back as soon as possible.

Dryw and I watched intently as her breathing became more erratic. During those last few moments of her life, we cried and continued to tell her how much we loved her. I told her again and again, "It's ok, it's ok. God is there for you. It's alright." And I tried to convey that we too would be okay.

Around 5:20 p.m. Shalita stopped breathing. As Dryw and I witnessed the inevitable, a wave of emotions roiled us. The dam broke, and we wailed as small rivers of tears ran down our faces. We prayed and said goodbye. Dryw and I held each other, shaking and weeping. My mind struggled to accept this new aching reality. *It's over, she's really gone.* Although I knew this moment would come, it still hit me like a punch in the stomach. *I've lost her. She is gone for good, and the dark and frightening life without her now begins.*

Not long after, Chris, John, Deana, Mom, and Daniel arrived. The next wave of tears came spilling down. After hours of weeping off and on, I was exhausted. I clearly remember that feeling, as if my batteries had been fully discharged. I was completely and utterly spent. It was a combination of fatigue, sleepiness, and sadness that I felt to my core. It was that strange feeling knowing that the woman I had loved for the last fourteen years, the mother of my boys, was gone forever. Only after I died would we reconnect. It was a feeling of sadness and aching like I had never known.

Friends come by; calls are made. People come and take my Baby Doll away.

Chapter 14

Saying Goodbye

About a week after Shalita's passing, we held her memorial service. It was somewhat of a blur. In preparation for the service, I went through hundreds of family photographs, including some from Shalita's childhood, and some just a few months old. I put the best ones together into a slide show to be shown at the end of the service. It was bittersweet combing through the images, but it was a project I threw myself into as I grieved.

Working with Chris and Deb, John and Deana, and Mom and our pastor, David George, we pulled together the plan for the service, being mindful of what Shalita would have wanted. I knew I wouldn't be in any shape to speak, but her brothers, Deb, my sister Susan and several close friends planned to speak.

I remember thinking that I didn't want to cry at the service. I thought that if I started I didn't know if I would be able to stop. I had had my moments in the days before the service, and while I knew there would be many more tears in the weeks and months ahead, there was something too public about crying there. And I wanted to be there for Daniel, Dryw, my mother-in-law, and the rest of the family.

After Pastor David George began the service, Chris spoke first, then John. I can only imagine how hard it was for them to talk about the passing of their little sister, whom they loved so dearly. Chris gave a loving and eloquent goodbye.

"I am Shalita's oldest brother, Chris Chitambar. Although we were separated by nine years, we were very close and shared a happy childhood made possible by loving, nurturing parents and family. Shalita, our brother, John, and I shared a lot in values that can only come from an upbringing rooted in faith and a belief in God.

There are not enough words in all the dictionaries in all the languages in the world to describe the pain, sorrow and loss that I feel. As I helplessly watched my beloved sister steadily succumb to her disease, every fiber in my being ached in grief for her. For the life she was losing, for the life she would never see, and for the emptiness that would be left behind in the lives of all those who loved her.

I mourned that I was losing not only a sister, but a close, wonderful friend whom I loved so very much. I even found myself bargaining, looking for every positive sign of improvement, even though I knew that the biology of her disease was such and what the outcome would be. We prayed for strength to get us through this time and for peace for Shalita.

But, our comings and goings, life and death are not in our hands. And amidst all the pain of losing her we are reminded that whether we live or die, we are the Lord's.

Shalita openly shared her Christian faith and love and devotion to God, touching many lives, including my own. And as I sat by her bedside reading her Bible, looking at all the verses she had underlined and the notes she had made, I was flooded with memories that ranged from her birth, and I am old enough to remember that day, to things we had said only days before. The memories of a lifetime are immense.

Shalita was a wonderful human being; she was beautiful inside and out. She touched our lives and gave selflessly of herself to others, forming deep relationships with those around her. I never cease to be amazed by the number of friends that she had. And, I heard this over and over again, she made everyone feel *as if* they were her best friend. It was truly a gift.

I want to share with you words from a letter that was sent to Shalita while she was in the hospital recently from Mary Winslow (the stepmother of one of Shalita's closest friends, Linda Clark).

"The first day I met you I realized what a special lady you were. The subsequent years have only reinforced my thinking. You are a blessing to all those who know you in any way at all."

Shalita felt that it was important to make events, whether they were with family or friends, into a memory that would last a long time. She was always talking about making a memory. Her life was way too short but it was rich with love. The center of which was her husband, Bill, and her boys Dryw and Daniel, and the rest of her family.

I will miss her smile, her touch, voice, her laughter, her music, her caring, and the many other things that went into her being truly, uniquely Shalita. Life will never be the same for me. But while our hearts ache we thank God for every day that our lives were blessed with this wonderful sister, daughter, wife, mother, aunt, and friend.

We love you, Shalita."

John spoke next. I watched as he struggled with his emotions, yet somehow stayed composed. His strong voice, laden with layers of pain, shared his stories.

"When my sister was born, I held her in my arms. And looking down at her lovingly I told her that we would give her the name Shalita. And when she grew up, when people would ask her 'who gave her that pretty name?' she would tell them her brother. I did not know what her name meant because I had made it up for my closest companion at that time, my rag doll.

My sister became my closest companion. Growing up we did everything together. We played, laughed, fought, cried, sang, danced. And when Shalita was 16 we both gave our hearts to God.

157

If I had one wish, and I know that my brother Chris joins me, if I had one wish for every brother, it would be to have a sister like Shalita. But there was only one Shalita and God gave her name the true meaning of love. His love, which she gave with all her heart to everyone she knew.

It will never seem fair that she was taken from us so early on in her life and that she had to suffer so. But I know that the loving, caring spirit of my sister will live on and heaven is richer because of her."

John then read a beautiful poem. After John my sister Susan spoke, followed by a few close friends. After the goodbyes, they showed the slide show I had put together. I remember seeing certain people there, many I hadn't seen in years, but the details are a blur. After the service our families and a few close friends came to my house, and it was good to spend time together as we all shared and suffered together.

A couple of Shalita's closest friends mentioned that they talked with a woman who had introduced herself as Shalita's best friend. They had never met this person and were taken aback at her claim to be Shalita's "best friend." They giggled at the notion that someone they hadn't met before or had heard of could be her best friend. But it was telling of Shalita's life and her relationships. Shalita had so many good friends, each one dear to her heart. Many marveled at the number of friends she had—from all walks of life. Friends from Sierra College and Sacramento State University, former students, friends from the cancer support group and the National Ovarian Cancer Coalition, friends from church, friends from UC Davis, and on and on.

In some ways traditional boundaries of family and friends blurred. Shalita treated her friends like family and she dearly loved her family, keeping in close contact like best friends. Making and keeping close relationships was truly one of her gifts.

From my journal

February 9, 2007
She's gone. It hurts so.

For weeks I said 'it's hard, it's really hard.' Tonight, though, as I listen to Chris Tomlin sing "How great is our God" for the thousandth time, the thoughts and feelings came down on me as I wept for the ten thousandth time, I thought 'it hurts,' and it does hurt so.

Pastor David George said I was a 'hero.' Tuesday Valerie Hall at work said I was 'incredible.' How foolish they sound. I am not a hero. I am just stumbling by each day, each hour and missing her so.

February 11, 2007
God, make me more like Shalita. Sweet, devoted, passionate, warm, smart, confident.

Dear Lord, hold my hand as I travel a path without my partner. Like Shalita's journey with cancer, a path I would not choose. Dan Link has been very caring and called often. I had lunch with Dave Robertson...

Dear Jesus, let me sleep and let me give this burden to you. Show me what you want for me – for me to do.

February 25, 2007
Shalita, fourteen years ago today I sat next to you and fell in love. I knew immediately you were someone very special. Before long I did love you, and, thankfully, you loved me.

My sweet darling, as I write to you and think of you my eyes well up with tears – there have been so many tears this month. You are the true love in my life, the only one I have really loved and now I miss you so.

You are an angel to me and so many others – and now – I can barely write – you are God's angel.

Comfort me, God, as I miss the lovely wife I knew, the mother of my children, the mother of Daniel and the mother of Dryw. Where are you? Are you here?

It is so hard to believe you are not here with me in our bedroom. The one we had remodeled. I can still see you in my mind reading in bed, telling me to take my shower.

You have a heart of gold, pure gold. Your love and sweetness are so deep, endless.

I am very sorry for not being more loving at times. For not holding you more, for being angry with you changing the house, for buying things. I was foolish and wrong, we never starved, we never ran low on money and I should have been more understanding.

I would give anything to take you to Salzburg as we discussed a few short months ago.

My dear Shalita, you touched so many lives and that is why so many are hurting now. My lovely angel, be near me, as I need you so. I am like a sailor on the vast ocean and feeling at times utterly lost. I feel despair that I may never see my home again.

Dryw and Daniel are doing alright, I think. They miss you terribly and I am trying hard to help them through this very difficult time. I will keep my promise, love – to love them and take the best care of them I can.

Mom is missing you terribly, of course, so we are all trying to look after her.

Please be near me and the boys, my love, ask God to carry us through each day, each fall and each time we reach out and you're not there. Please ask God to give me wisdom, encouragement, compassion and strength. I feel so weak at times.

My dear Shalita, you are so beautiful, so loving and kind, so wise, yet so understanding. Thank you for being very supportive to me these last 14 years. Thank you for saying yes to see Bruce Carroll (in concert) on March 10, 1993, for sticking with me in June and July 1993, when things were rocky between us, for saying yes on December 11, 1993, and for saying "I do" on June 18, 1994. And thank you for always sticking with me through our hard times.

As I said many times – you are the best, and I will never, ever forget you – how could I? You are a big part of me. I love you very, very much.

Your Bill

One day in early March, I began reading one of her journals. I had glanced at a few briefly over the years, but never really sat down to read them. I wanted to respect her privacy and, frankly, it wasn't something I had thought much about until that day. Over the next few weeks I began reading them and found more tucked away in her closet and dresser.

I began to realize that journaling was her way of sharing some of her most intimate times with God. There was both a constancy of yearning for God and also an aching deep within her for God to maintain that intimacy. It was then I realized that, despite all the time we had spent together in the last fourteen years, there was a part of her that I had not fully known. It was there, perhaps veiled at times, but I failed to fully recognize it, to fully grasp her thirst for a deeper relationship with God. *Was this always present in Shalita, or had I just missed it?*

Over the next few weeks, I began to hunt for other journals. While I had noticed that she had spent a lot of time journaling, I didn't realize that there were so many.

March 6, 2007

I read Shalita's journal today. It's one of many and covers all of 1993 and up to 1997. It was so satisfying to read in parts – about how we met, began dating, our challenges over summer and engagement and wedding. It was hard in parts to read, but such a joy mostly. Her journals make my entries pale in comparison. She had such spiritual depth.

Dear God – see me through this painful course. You have carried me this far. Help me be more like her, Lord, and even more so like you, Jesus! Help me be more disciplined. Lay men before me with Godly wisdom. Take my eyes off worldly things and false beauties. How weak I am. I do love you too, Lord, and bless my sweet, sweet Shalita in your kingdom. Ease the pain I feel, Mom C. feels, Dryw feels, Daniel feels, Chris feels, John feels and many, many dear friends.

I thank you greatly, dear Lord, for giving me a wife that brought me such joy and companionship and gives me strength and confidence today – still. Bless our boys and help me to be a better father and son. Heal the hurts in our family and bring those in the family that don't know you back to the church.

In the months that followed, as I continued to read her writings and seek more glimpses of her past life, I stumbled upon her earliest journals. There, on the top shelf of our walk-in closet, I peered up one day and saw two familiar boxes decorated in bold pink-and-white floral designs, *classic Shalita*. I carefully reached up on the white painted shelf where they had resided undisturbed for years and pulled each box down. I rummaged through them and found mostly greeting cards people had sent her over the years. But among the collection of cards and notes I found three small journals from her childhood. My heart raced. They spanned from 1969 to 1977, and were sure to provide me new insight into these early formative years.

Later that week, as I was about to leave for work, I began to read one of her childhood journals. It was a very small, thin booklet with a pink paper book cover. On the front it had her name, address in

Madison, Wisconsin, and at the bottom written in large letters: PRIVATE.

I carefully opened its fragile pages. Inside it read: "Notes on the things we see and do." This earliest of her journals chronicled her family's travels and coming to the US in 1969. It contained simple descriptions of her travels that year.

Thurs. 8th
Started to Lucknow at 7:15. The journey was long and hot. Reached Lucknow 11 o'clock. Went straight to Aunty Dolly's place, washed up and went to Uncle Archie's place for lunch . . .

Sat. 18th
Got up 4 o'clock, went to Calcutta by the coal fueled express. Reached there at 10 am. Went to Wellington Square by taxi . . .

Tues. 21st
7 o'clock flew to London by Kuwait Airway. It was very pretty. The crew was nice. Flew 5000 miles per hour. It was a 17 hour journey. Stopped at Dubai and Kuwait. Stopped at Athens and bought a souvenir doll. Then at Geneva, flew over the Swiss Alps. Like a dream. We came back to the plane after our stop in Geneva (and) discovered they had disposed of our souvenirs, which Mummy put in the air sickness bag. Reached London. It was so cold and damp. We went straight to Tonbridge.

As I read the simple log of her journeys, I thought of a precocious little girl back in India. I began to think: what would ten-year-old Shalita Chitambar think of her husband reading this and her other journals, many more detailed and intimate, some forty years later? Would she be delighted or embarrassed? Would she want her thoughts shared with the world? As I silently pondered these questions, it struck me that I was prying off sheets of plywood from a home that had long been shuttered. I was peeling back layers of a private world that no one else had witnessed. The questions I found myself asking I could not answer, but I was thrilled with each new discovery of her writings.

Chapter 15

Coping

Those first weeks after Shalita's passing, I felt and saw her everywhere. In the evening, I could picture her lying in bed. "You should take your shower, honey" I could hear her say. And later, her still reading, I would say, "Turn out the lights, Babe." "Two more minutes," would be her reply. In the morning I would wake up and for a few seconds, feeling normal, and then the sharp pain of remembering came back. That she was gone and how she had suffered those last months.

Seeing her picture was an obvious physical reminder of her, and when I saw one, it brought strong feelings of affection, and, at the same time, it poked hard at my tender wound. There were so many things in our house—a house she took pride in decorating and arranging—that I associated with her. Some remembrances came with a small twinge of sadness, and others pummeled me.

One afternoon in late February I walked into my bathroom and closed the door. I looked up and saw a long, white terrycloth robe hanging on a hook behind the door. Her robe. I froze. Weeks had gone by, how had I missed it? I could see Shalita slipping it on after her shower.

She had bought the robe in Las Vegas in October 2005, when we went on a trip with her brothers and sisters-in-law. We did the touristy thing and walked the strip, enjoyed excellent food at the Bellagio, and caught a show. We stayed at the MGM, lounging by the pool in robes from our room. Shalita and I had decided to buy ours and bring them home as souvenirs. As I stood there, staring at the silly robe, paralyzed, all the poignant memories of the trip came rushing back and pounded me.

And then came the familiar dates—May 4th was Shalita's birthday; days later came Mother's day. June 18th was our anniversary. August 23rd was the day she was diagnosed. There was the day we had learned of her recurrence, the day we first met, the holidays, the day she died. There was no escape. The calendar was filled with important touchstones of our lives, our story together. And now mine was divided into distinct partitions: before cancer diagnosis (August 2004), remission and recurrence (June 2006), and after her death.

From my journal

April 23, 2007
Each morning I lay in bed not ready to rise, feeling empty inside. I don't want to get up, much like when I'm in the shower. I just want the hot water to continue – like a warm blanket I can be comforted in, I can be secure. I feel inside that it will ease the hurt, but I know it won't.

When I see your picture I touch it, I stroke your cheek like I used to stroke your face. I was listening to Michael McDonald's "All Is Fair in Love." The feelings came back, washing over me. As I tried to sit and stretch and meditate I could see you, Shalita, as clear as I see this pen and paper. We sat looking at each other. Your beautiful dark brown eyes looked into mine. We held hands and then held each other so tightly. I wept. 3 months.

***

I found myself going over various situations in my head, asking *What if?* It was an affliction. I would recount the course of events that eventually led to Shalita's death by playing out hypothetical scenarios: What if Dr. Teymouri had taken more tests in the spring of 2004? Since ovarian cancer is considered a hormonal cancer, would it have been different if we had had another child after Daniel? Would it have delayed it? What if Dr. Scudder, her oncologist at UC Davis Medical Center, had told us about the tumors on her spine in November 2006, as he should have? Would they have been able to do radiation and control her pain better? Would it have extended her life? What if she had eaten differently, would it have mattered?

These were, of course, questions that couldn't be answered. It was a pointless exercise that invariably left me frustrated and

166

depressed. But I think it was a normal, perhaps unavoidable, part of grieving for me. I also knew that too much ruminating on the "what ifs" was not healthy or helpful. I had to let go of past things that could have been or might have happened. As I saw how empty I felt at the end of this cycle, I began making a conscious effort to stop those thoughts before they ran their full course.

In the weeks after her passing, I began to slowly realize what this new life would be like without my loving wife. I remember several days after her death suddenly realizing that I was now a single dad. It was a painful, somewhat strange revelation. It shouldn't have been, because it had been clear for weeks that Shalita was going to die. I didn't know if it was going to be in January or later that year, but all signs showed no other path. It shouldn't have been something I thought of only after her death, but it was. I hated the idea of telling people I was a single dad. In my mind single moms and single dads were divorced people. I wasn't divorced.

There were other things that should have been obvious but also came as painful revelations, like what to do with Daniel when he was out of school and I was still at work. And, several weeks later, what was I going to do with him over the summer break? My mind had been so focused on taking care of the boys and worrying about Shalita and her care that I hadn't thought much about the future. I wasn't prepared for the transition that I now found myself going through.

***

In mid-February I decided I would go through her clothes. I planned to give some clothes to family and friends and donate the rest. To Shalita, clothes were a *passion*. She loved buying them, and her packed walk-in closet revealed this simple truth. If clothes shopping were an Olympic event, Shalita would have easily made the finals. There wasn't a Ross, T.J. Maxx, Marshalls, or Nordstrom Rack within twenty miles of our home that she didn't know intimately. Coldwater Creek and Chico's were among her favorite sources for jackets, blouses, pants, and jewelry.

To me, her clothing collection was a bit of an irritation. While I admired Shalita for caring how she dressed and looked, her clothes shopping, which at times bordered on obsessive, went counter to my sensibilities of saving money. She was the spender and I was the saver. We often discussed this and usually agreed on strategies to strike a balance between her desire to buy things and my desire to put money away for the future. But agreement rarely turned into results that achieved that balance.

The process of moving out her clothes, I knew, would be emotional. But I told myself I could handle it. I was wrong. In fact I was completely unprepared for the experience. Something about letting go of her clothes was far more complicated and emotionally laden than I had imagined. Every time I opened the closet door, alarms would go off in my head and a profound sadness would envelop me. I couldn't even look at the closet without stirring up a strong ache that ran deep inside me. It was as if her closet had an invisible force field around it and as much as I tried, I couldn't break through.

For many months I kept the closet door closed and left it alone. Eventually I gave away some of her clothes to friends and family. But it was more than three years after her passing that I finally completed the job of giving away the last of her clothes. I felt a relief when it was done, but somewhat a bit ashamed that it took me so long.

While processing my grief and trying to take good care of myself, I knew I had to make sure that Daniel, who was ten at the time, was okay. Immediately following Shalita's death, Daniel didn't show a lot of emotion. I don't think I saw him cry, and I wasn't sure what to make of it, but I knew he was surely grieving in his own way. *Certainly kids process things differently than adults*, I told myself. I watched him carefully over the next several months. At the suggestion of Sutter Hospital's Hospice program, Daniel worked with a child therapist that used art as a means of helping kids through their grief. He saw the therapist about five times and although he showed some resistance to working with her, I felt that, over time, it would be beneficial to him.

One evening in early June I got a glimpse of some of the pain he felt losing his mother. I was working on the computer in our study and had put Daniel to bed about fifteen minutes earlier, when I heard him shuffle through the door. As I turned around I saw tears streaming down his face. "I miss Mommy," he blurted out. I was a little stunned, and didn't know what had triggered this reaction or what to do. I reached out my arms. He came to me, and as I held him tightly the tears continued, as if he couldn't hold in these feelings any longer.

It was unexpected. While it broke my heart to see him grieving this way, it was also reassuring to see him let these painful emotions out. I think what had touched off those emotions was, in part, the time of year. The summer was traditionally a very exciting time for Daniel, as he was out of school, and would spend much more time with his mom while she was on her summer break. This year it would be different. Over the next few months there were similar words and emotions, although less intense.

It was also hard for me to read how Dryw was doing with the loss of his mother. While we had both cried when she died, he was then twenty years old and was extremely busy. Whether at school, with friends, or with his band, I rarely saw him, especially because he often came home after I was asleep. In September 2007, I remember him coming home one evening while I finished watching a movie. We chatted briefly and somehow the discussion turned to his mom. He explained that he still had a voicemail message from her and couldn't bring himself to delete it. She had called him while she was in the hospital, wanting him to come visit her. She sounded angry, Dryw said, because he hadn't spent much time with her in the hospital. As he shared this with me he began to cry. It was the first time since her death I had seen him cry. I explained that his mother loved him very much and that he shouldn't feel bad. As with Daniel, it was good to see him let go of some of the emotions, which I think in many ways he had been holding inside.

Chapter 16

The Long Fall

As the reality of my new life without Shalita settled in, I expected the first year would be very difficult. The road ahead would surely be a bumpy one, and I told myself to just hang on and get through the next twelve months. But along with the emotional pain I felt in those first months, my body also began to throw me some unexpected curves.

One evening in July, I felt some pain in my left foot while on a walk around the neighborhood. I thought it was my shoes, but a few days later I woke up and could barely walk. My left foot was swollen and shooting pain coursed through me when I tried putting weight on it. I saw my doctor, who thought it was gout. He sent me out for a blood test to confirm his diagnosis and referred me to a podiatrist. The podiatrist also thought it was gout, and put me on anti-inflammatories. However, the blood test came back negative for gout. Whatever it was, the pain and swelling were intense for a few weeks. During much of 2007 there were several new aches and pains. It seemed pretty clear to me that it was my body's way of protesting, of speaking out. "*Enough,*" it was saying, "*I can't take it!*"

Sometime during that restless summer, I remember walking past Daniel's room and noticing it was a huge mess. While this was nothing new or surprising, it looked particularly bad that day, and it really bothered me. Aggravated, I walked in and started picking up things around the room. Clothes on the floor, toys scattered here and there; all assortments of Daniel's life were strewn around the room. Pulling the bed away from the wall was the worst. A plethora of candy wrappers, dirty socks, soda cans—seemingly everything he had touched in the last three months—was there. It was unbelievable the stuff he had shoved under his bed. The closet was also a disaster. *How can I live like this? How can he live like this?*

As I worked to put clothes away, I noticed that the drawers in his dresser were difficult to open and close. While fooling around with the sticky drawers, it occurred to me that they had gotten mixed up and were not in the right sequence. This small, common oak chest had four drawers, and while it was not obvious, each one was a slightly different size. The mixed-up drawers were hard to use. I took each drawer out and emptied the contents into a pile. Next, I methodically tried each drawer in the spaces until I had them all in their correct slots.

As I weeded out the candy wrappers and knickknacks, filling up the drawers with socks, underwear and shirts, something struck me. This mismatched dresser was a metaphor for my life. On the surface I looked pretty much the same as a year or two before. I lived in the same house, attended the same church, and disappeared each morning to go do the same job. But on the inside, things were different. I was a mess. My mind, body, and soul felt lost. The pain and chaos of my life had turned my world upside down. The drawers of life were all there, just as before, but each had been randomly shoved into its space and filled with whatever was within reach to throw in.

By August I felt physically and mentally worn down. I began experiencing episodes of intense anxiety. I decided to see Shalita's primary care physician, Kandell Judge. Originally from India, Dr. Judge was tall and possessed an inviting smile. Whenever we received troubling medical news about Shalita's health, Dr. Judge had a way of lightening the gloom we were feeling. Shalita really liked her and the two had quickly bonded. Although I sometimes felt a little like a fifth wheel when I went with Shalita to see her, I thought a visit to her office might do me good.

As I sat in her examining room, I wondered if she would remember me. When she opened the door she looked up and gave me a broken smile and paused, tears welling up. She stepped forward and gave me a long hug. "I have never been so affected by one of my patients before. I really miss your wife." I also got choked up, and we spent the first couple of minutes catching up. It felt good being able to talk with her about Shalita, and also to talk with her about how I was doing. I told her about my aches and pains, and then explained how a recent trip to Santa Cruz with Daniel had brought on a wave of intense anxiety. I distinctly recall how paralyzed and out of control I felt over the course of that weekend.

After a lengthy description of my situation, Dr. Judge told me a story. She said that when she was a little girl growing up in India she was walking home from school one day and encountered a snake. It was a deadly cobra. She was able to avoid it and quickly made it safely home. Some hours later some men came by the house and said that they had killed the cobra. After hearing this she completely broke down. It was an intense reaction, even though her encounter had been hours earlier. "Stress is like that sometimes," she explained. "It can hit hours or even many months later. What you experienced," she continued, "is a delayed response to Shalita's death." She was telling me that I was likely experiencing PTSD—post-traumatic stress disorder. Dr. Judge had several useful suggestions on dealing with the anxiety, and I found it helpful to share with her what I was experiencing and hearing her perspective.

Over the next few months, I slowly began to feel emotionally and physically stronger. By the end of 2007, for the first time, I felt like the emotional clouds were beginning to lift and my outlook was improving. But life wasn't done throwing me curves, and 2008 came on strong with many challenges.

***

In February 2008, I took a chance and changed jobs. After more than fifteen years with the Energy Commission, I moved to the California Air Resources Board (ARB), a sister state agency. I had loved my job at the Energy Commission, but that job involved multiple meetings a day, seemingly endless emails, and managing a staff of 11. I was also frustrated with the pay disparity between my job and the equivalent of a job in the private sector, so I was ready for a change. But as is often true with job changes, the transition was stressful.

It was about this time that my dad's health began to decline. Born in Chattanooga, Tennessee, shortly after World War I, my father was somewhat of a loner but an outdoor enthusiast. He and a handful of others formed the Southern California Chapter of the Sierra Club in 1956, and he continued to pursue his passion of hiking in the Sierra Nevada Mountains whenever he could. As a child I was dragged along for many of these hikes, and it was this exposure to the beauty of the Sierra Mountains that years later would influence me toward a path in the environmental field.

After my mom died in 2004, Dad understandably struggled. In 2006, he was diagnosed with pulmonary fibrosis, a serious and progressive lung disease. It was a shock to all of us, but Dad seemed to handle it fairly well and remained strong as an ox, both physically and mentally. While he was very concerned about his health, he was determined to go out kicking. It was this attitude and stubbornness that both kept him going, but also drove my siblings and me a little nuts at times.

As his condition worsened in early 2008, he began to suffer shortness of breath and was no longer able to hike or go on long walks. This was very hard for him since I always saw this outlet as his unique brand of therapy. By that summer, he was on oxygen most of the time and was in and out of the hospital for infections and a variety of symptoms related to the fibrosis.

One day, in the summer of 2008, I was in a meeting at work with a few high-level people from ARB and the California Environmental Protection Agency, ARB's parent agency. After the meeting a woman I knew casually and had worked with came up to me to chat. "How are you doing?" she asked. I fumbled for a response and said that I was okay. She had obviously heard about Shalita and, in her own strange way, was trying to see how I was doing. "You look terrible," she blurted out.

I knew that she could be blunt, but I was a not prepared for that biting comment. What could I say? Certainly the stress had taken a toll. With my own health problems and having lost some weight, I wasn't the picture of health. Part of me bristled at her rudeness, but part of me was resigned to this cold fact. She was right.

With the challenges of the new job, seeing Dad decline, and struggling with my own health issues, I began slipping deeper into depression. Along with the depression came powerful waves of anxiety, which both frustrated and frightened me. Simple things became a huge effort. At work, the mundane became painful. At home, seemingly menial tasks, like picking up the study, just didn't get done. I was either physically exhausted from episodes of fatigue or I just couldn't bring myself to jump in and finish a job. The tasks that didn't get done made me feel more depressed and I felt the weight of unfinished business was beginning to pile up on me.

***

By November 2008, my nerves were about as stable as an old stick of TNT. And then I hit bottom. I found my bouts with anxiety worsening. Not just anxiety, but with a heavy dose of depression and with increasing frequency. When anxiety surfaced, which could last anywhere between an afternoon to a few days, there were telltale signs that would recur. Symptoms (manifestations) included extreme irritability, heightened sensitivity to sights and sounds, ruminations, intense worry over small things, and some very disturbing thoughts. Anything and everything would set me off. This mainly happened at home. I would be walking down the hall and I would see a crumb on the floor. Instead of stopping, bending over and picking it up, and throwing it away, it would rattle me. Instead my mind would spiral, thinking: *This place is a mess. What am I going to do?* If I picked it up, then I would inevitably then see a small piece of paper, a leaf fragment, or some other piece of debris on the floor and I would pick those up too. But it didn't stop there, I would see something else that needed to be taken care of, like dirty dishes or a spot on the kitchen cabinet, and I felt compelled to take on another small chore, then another.

After a short time it would completely throw me off track of whatever I was originally doing. It was exhausting, and I knew that I was fighting a losing battle. There would always be something in the house that needed cleaning or fixing. There would always be things to throw away and calls to be made, and it would start what I would call *spinning*. The spinning moved to other areas of my life, too, such as my health. Thoughts like this would naturally upset me, but instead of examining the thought that my health was only getting worse and worse and recognizing that aches and pains naturally come and go over time, these thoughts grew into anxieties that would completely color my view on the future. It was as if life would be an unstoppable slide downhill, and in that moment, my mind was certain that life would be more and more painful until I died. I couldn't see any blue sky through the gray clouds.

Strangely, another symptom I experienced during this period of anxiety was some kind of "amazing insight," in which I would have moments of great wisdom, or so I thought. An idea would come in my head, and I would think, *Wow, I've never thought of that before!* Or, *I hadn't realized that until this very moment.* These thoughts and ideas, I was convinced, were truly profound. I felt a real sense of enlightenment. I also believed with absolutely certainty that sharing these new insights would be incredibly helpful to others. They would pop up frequently, like watching shooting stars on an August night... *There's one, look, there's another one.* And just as oddly as these "amazing insights" popped in my head, they would evaporate just as quickly as they came. To this day, I cannot remember one of the "revelations" that I experienced during that time.

I also found it difficult to make decisions. This, I came to learn, is a common symptom of depression. I found myself tormented over both large and small decisions. Once a decision was made, I often second-guessed myself, dwelling over details and hypothetical outcomes. The simplest decisions could paralyze me.

As my anxiety grew noticeably worse, I experienced thoughts of hurting myself or others. It's hard to say exactly the roots of these dark thoughts, but certainly it was more evidence that my mind was becoming overwhelmed from years of loss and the associated intense stress. While driving, I would have flashes of crossing the line and plowing head on into on-coming traffic. I found myself having to put all of my focus on staying calm and even began to drive toward the right side of my lane. Heights absolutely terrified me. If I walked near a rail with a large drop, I would have visions of jumping to my death. Much like my driving episodes, I would have to put all of my energy into keeping myself calm.

When these tidal waves of fear struck, it was torture. This was by far the worst of the symptoms I experienced. At times I felt possessed with these deeply disturbing thoughts and they were terrifying. Once these dark thoughts crept into my mind, it was very difficult to shake them. Worse, although I had no desire to hurt or kill others or myself, I honestly couldn't say that I wouldn't follow through. I began to wonder if I was losing my sanity and if I would be able to care for Daniel and myself. *What about my job?* I thought, *Could I continue to hold down a job? What about this house? Who will care for my Daniel if I am not fit to parent him? How will he handle the losses of his mother and a father that went off the deep end?* It was a very difficult and disturbing road I found myself on.

July 30, 2008

Dearest Lord Jesus, watch over this family – broken in part by the loss of our lovely Shalita. Heavenly Father, heal my stomach, my back and my lonely heart. Open my eyes to the beauty and richness you provide. Free me of impure thoughts, envy, anger and greed. How weak am I and well aware of your love for me, despite my failures, doubts and weakness.

Send my love to Shalita and keep her near as our own guardian angel. Bring her presence and love to Dryw, Daniel and me. Let us feel and know her loving arms around us.

Lord, heal Chris as he lays in a hospital room recovering from his heart attack and surgery. Strengthen Deb as she cares for him.

Jesus, help me to know how to love more, how to see things as you would, and help me honor you, and feel the peace and confidence that you alone can give. Let me leave the world of shallowness and grow tall and strong in your truth.

September 22, 2008

Argh! My mind has a . . . (self) of its own. My stomach hurts, foot hurts, etc., etc.

(But) God is good. I hope to see Dr. Bisharat at 4 pm to see if I can get a referral and antianxiety medication.

The dirty, bug-laden kitchen/house and yard frustrate me. I know I am expecting too much – especially from Dryw and Daniel.

Dear Lord and ruler above, heal my aching heart, my troubled body, my racing mind. You alone are holy and I must trust you now and place my complete confidence and faith in you!

Dear Jesus, please walk with me and keep my path straight.

Holy Spirit, do an awesome healing in all of me. Allow me to loosen my grip.

Dear Lord, let me count my many blessings, even now as I struggle!

- For your Son Jesus
- For loving me
- For showing my worthiness when I am discouraged
- Valley Springs Presbyterian Church . . .

***

As I struggled with the ongoing anxiety and depression during the fall of 2008, my dad's health was rapidly deteriorating. I felt physically worn down and barely in control of my thoughts and actions. One Sunday evening in December, I went to check on my dad at his house. He was connected to his oxygen tank through a long, meandering tube that ran through much of the house. To my surprise I found him bundled up in a heavy jacket. The house was surprisingly warm, as Dad typically kept his house fairly cool in winter (he was of the mind that as little as possible should be spent on necessities like food, clothes, and utilities). He asked me to turn up the heat, and when I did I saw that the thermostat was at 76 degrees. I couldn't understand why he was so cold. "Dad, what have you eaten today?" "Not much," he replied. "I had some toast for lunch." I told him that he was feeling so cold because he hadn't eaten enough. I found a can of chicken noodle soup in the garage pantry and heated it up for him. He thanked me and ate the soup and some other food I prepared for him. After we talked a little more, I told him I needed to go home to put Daniel to bed.

Dad was now on oxygen all day and night and I worried about him tripping over the long tube connected to the tank. It was clear that he was in no condition to take care of himself all alone in his house. Not only was his condition progressing, he seemed to be confused as well. At one point he put his weary hands down on the table and, with an awful look of resignation on his face, proceeded to slowly lower his head on them. I pleaded with him to let me call someone to help him and, as he had for months, he again resisted my suggestion. "No, I'll be fine," he said, his head still bowed resting on his hands.

I can still see Dad that day, in his forest green down jacket with his head of thinning, gray hair plopped on the table. While I didn't realize it at the time, at that exact moment something deep in the recesses of my brain snapped. Here was the man who had survived the Battle of the Bulge, who was taken prisoner by the Germans during World War II, and survived to tell about it. A man, who up until a month or two before, was stronger than most men in their thirties or forties. Now it seemed he could collapse at any minute, and yet he still refused to let someone help him, to let me help him. It was too much for my weary psyche. It was the proverbial last straw on the camel's back.

I worried if he would make it through the next week or two; I didn't even know if he would make it through the night. And yet, I was thinking: *This is what he wanted, wasn't it, to die at home?* Reluctantly, I left. When I arrived home, I remember feeling extremely irritable. I immediately snapped at Daniel for some minor reason, I don't remember why. I knew I needed to stay away from Daniel, because I felt like I was going to explode. The last thing I wanted was to yell at Daniel, or worse.

The next day I dragged myself to work. It was Monday, and I had met an old friend for lunch. Michelle Edwards and I had both been tour guides at the State Capitol in the mid- to late 1980s. She eventually became my boss, and we had gotten along very well. As Michelle and I talked I told her all of the things I was dealing with— grief for Shalita, concern over my physical and mental health, and now my dad's failing health. I think she sensed it as much as I did that I was near a breaking point.

Later that day I attended a large meeting at work. It was mostly supervisors and midlevel managers that met every other Monday to discuss the status of activities in the climate change program I was working in. My job was merely to listen and take notes; I had no role that day in presenting or answering questions. The meeting began at three p.m. and lasted about an hour. After the first few minutes I found myself completely preoccupied with Dad's worsening condition, and I doubt that I took in any more than a few words during entire the meeting. As thoughts and worries bounced around in my head, I felt an intense wave of anxiety welling up in me.

It was like a thermometer in a pot of water about to boil. The little voices in my head grew louder.

About twenty minutes into the meeting, completely oblivious at this point to what was being discussed, my brain said *ENOUGH!* I wanted to scream—literally. A primal scream was rising from deep within me. I was so completely overwhelmed that an internal battle broke out in my head. I felt paralyzed as part of me said *SCREAM, Bill! You've been through enough, just let it out.* That thought, of course, clashed with the rational side of my brain, which was saying: *Don't you dare scream out loud! What will people think?* I could hear the gossip already: "Did you hear about the guy who lost his wife and one day, in the middle of a big meeting he hollered at the top of his lungs? Can you imagine? He just lost it."

The epic battle in my head raged on, and it took all of my effort to control my voice and to keep quiet. As the meeting began to wind down, I realized that I was going to make it through the meeting without completely freaking out, but I knew something inside me had snapped and I needed help right then. When the meeting ended I turned to my boss, Jon, who I'm sure was completely unaware of the torture I was going through, and told him I didn't feel well and needed to go home. He said fine, wished me well, and I quickly walked out of the room.

The only thing I could think of that would help me in my state of near incapacitation was to call my counselor, Carol. I had been seeing Carol for the past couple of months and she was the only person I could think of that would know what to do, that would understand. My sanity was hanging by a thread and it felt like the slightest puff of wind would send me plummeting into the abyss. I pulled out my cell phone and called Carol. I left her a message and thankfully she called me right back. She could fit me in at five p.m.— just an hour away.

Something deep inside me, it seemed, was telling me I had to escape. I had to escape Dad, I had to escape work, I had to let go of my responsibilities at home. I headed out the door on my way to see Carol, but as soon as I left the building my body began to shake. I had to take a light-rail train to get to my car before I could drive to Carol's office, and in my frazzled state, I called my sister Susan. Over the next hour she talked with me and coached me as I road the train to my car and from my car to Carol's office. My brain was spinning, and was so overwhelmed at that point that I began to lose touch with what was real and logical. During the drive to Carol's office, I became convinced I could predict the future. It was one of the weirdest experiences of my life. I could barely drive, but somehow I made it to the office.

As soon as I saw Carol I burst into tears. The dam had broken. As I recounted my tortured mental state, she listened intently. We both agreed I needed to take a break from work and life in general. Over the next week and a half, I took off time from work and participated in fairly intensive therapy. It was an emotional time, and at times terrifying. But the therapy was cathartic in helping me to let go and ultimately led me to a deeper understanding of all that I was dealing with. The levels of anxiety and stress over the previous six months had left me about ten pounds lighter and my thin body couldn't afford to lose that much weight. Fortunately, the weight I had lost all came back over the course of four or five weeks. This was no small feat for me, as in the past, it was difficult and very slow for me to put on weight. But after I took time off from work and temporarily shed many of my daily responsibilities, I suddenly had my appetite back.

By late December my dad was back in the hospital, this time for several weeks. And while he looked better and was upbeat during most of his stay, he realized that he wasn't going to improve much and that his lung condition was running its course. On January 17, 2009, five years and one day after my mother passed, my father died. It was a peaceful and quick ending to a lengthy battle with his disease. He died at home, and my siblings and I think it was no coincidence that he died within hours of the five-year anniversary of Mom's passing.

Within that five-year period I had now lost both parents, my father-in-law, and my wife. I had witnessed each of them taking their last earthly breaths, and while I had not experienced a physical war, my mind and body were suffering battle fatigue.

March 3, 2009
Forty-five minutes ago it became apparent that I have a cold. This is a mere inconvenience compared to my depression, anxiety, paranoia, etc. Dad's decline was hard, for me especially . . . (I've spent) three or four weeks at Heritage

Oaks Partial Outpatient program and tomorrow I return. I have been taking (medications for the anxiety and depression) . . . It is so upsetting and painful.

Dear Lord, heal my mind, my ailing body. Wash my sins away and open my eyes to your truth and goodness. Heal, too, my broken heart that longs for my sweet Shalita. Protect this home and the boys from any serious harm. Put in our paths believers that can support us as we stumble. Open my heart again to the hurting masses as the world economies crack and fail.

Dear God my Father in Heaven, keep close the Blackburns, Chitambars and Owens. Bring them into your fold if it's your will. Do this for the Helmans (my sister Susan's family) too.

Father, I thank you for Dryw and Daniel, for Mom C. for Susan and Lori and friends. You have blessed me with fair health, a good home, a sense of humor, a good mind, more things and money than I need. Thank you also for (my job at ARB and friends there) . . .

May 31, 2009
My moods have been mixed. Good for a week or two then (it falls). Battling blues and anxiety. The anxiety manifests itself in becoming upset or irritable over the smallest things (small mess at home, etc.).

At this moment Daniel is playing the drums in his room and his new friend Jade is playing his electric guitar – quite the pair (watch out Dryw, they're right behind you!).

A good day. Mood good to very good. I am blessed by Mom C. ("you're looking better"), Dryw and his thoughtfulness and Danny's affection and generosity. Thank you Lord for Susan's time and care, Chris and Deb, etc., etc. (Lynn Hutchinson too!)

September 9, 2009

Heavenly Father, you have carried me far. Gone are the disturbing thoughts – the worst thing ever – and my moods are more often up. Please protect Dryw and me from frivolous lawsuits [resulting from an accident Dryw was in] and your will be done. Heal Daniel from this cold and imprint your message of salvation and mercy on his heart. Bless Dryw and Katherine – let them know if and when to marry. Keep Dryw growing as he has been! Please help Daniel to be neater. Bless Lori and heal her. Show me what to do and not do.

December 31, 2009

Dear heavenly Father, touch me now as my mind is "spinning." Anxiety has crept back, please push it out . . . In Jesus' name. Amen

Although my thoughts race, although I second-guess most thoughts, feelings and ideas, although my view of my own worth rises and falls like a child, God is good and is Bigger than this (too)!

I read Grandpa Bickford's letter to me just now. It's dated May 9, 1966 – just days before his death. I realize at this moment that it's one of the most special things I have and am grateful for it. It's as if he wrote it for me to read today, 43 ½ years later. (It calms my racing mind and makes him more near now – when I need him.)

Dryw and Daniel are doing whatever on the computer. It's nice to have Dryw here. I wouldn't want to be alone, tonight especially. I want to write more to get more out, but my will and thoughts fall short.

***

By the spring of 2009, a little more than two years after Shalita's death, I began to slowly climb out of the mental hole I had found myself in. It was a slow and rocky recovery. I was told that I would likely continue to deal with episodes of depression and its effects, but as the year progressed, I began to feel physically and emotionally stronger. In 2010, I started to move past basic survival, and began to have some fun again. I became more involved with yoga, which both relaxed me and helped ease some of my back pain. I joined Arthur Murray Dance Studio and began to attend dances. While I learned slowly, frustratingly so at times, dancing was and continues to be a joy and has opened up a world I had largely viewed from the sidelines. Getting back into a Bible study, which Shalita and I had enjoyed doing together, was also very important for me, as I had missed those times and longed for the closeness and intimacy of a small study group. I found the fellowship and a sense of community, in particular, very valuable.

As I began to reflect on the losses and intense stress I experienced over the last several years, it was clear that several areas of my life had been deeply affected. My health issues were challenging, and several areas of my life where I felt some measure of control and influence had also been diminished. Leaving my job as a supervisor to take on a staff position at the Air Resources Board meant I now had very little say in day-to-day decisions. I was no longer in a role where I made decisions hiring, training, and directing staff. While I didn't miss the intensity and pressure I sometimes felt in supervising, I very much missed my staff. I also missed having a measure of control and responsibility of my work and the work of others. Despite my many years of experience, I didn't feel particularly valued in my current position.

The preceding seven years of loss and change had taken a heavy toll. Each loss was like a small fire taking out part of a forest. Individually, their damage was limited, but cumulatively the destruction was far more widespread. And when the rains came, as they always do, the topsoil washed down the hill because the trees, shrubs, and underbrush were gone. Little was left to hold the soil in place. But unlike the forest, which regenerates after fire and heavy rains, I sensed that my body was never going to return to the level of health I had previously, and that I desperately wanted back.

After Shalita's diagnosis with cancer, she talked about her new life, post cancer. In some of her talks she referred to it as "Act II." My Act II was the day Shalita died, some thirty months after her grim diagnosis. It was the beginning of a difficult new chapter, one without my precious partner.

But I realized—just as Shalita had—that when you lose your old life, new opportunities surely follow. These new opportunities offered hope and exciting possibilities.

Chapter 17

Shalita's Gifts

Shalita, 2004

While the path has been a difficult one, I have grown in many important ways during the last several years. Being single again meant getting back into the kitchen, which I continue to enjoy. Ballroom dancing lessons, something I had always wanted to do, was a great new activity as well, and, in the process of learning to make my way around the dance floor, I made several new friends.

The changes that occurred in my life did lead to growth, just as I had desperately hoped for when Shalita's prognosis was bleak, and while I began to experience gradual personal growth through the many changes that occurred, it was only through time, support from families and friends, and leaning heavily on God, that I began to realize some gradual healing.

Over time I began to see that, while Shalita was physically gone, she had left me with many incredible blessings and gifts in my life. At the very time I was experiencing the worst of my depression and anxiety, I realized something profound—how very fortunate I was. Through my pain the bigger picture became very clear—Shalita had given me some truly amazing gifts; ones that would last a lifetime.

Shalita had not only given me the tremendous gifts of Dryw and Daniel; she had also given me her entire loving family. While her mother and brothers went through their own intense grieving after her death, they were very supportive to the boys and me. So, too, were sisters-in-law Deb and Deana. Then I thought about Shalita's many friends; some of her closest friends were now my friends and were a huge help to my family. In particular, Shalita's Sierra College colleagues Roselene and Clare, and their husbands Dick and Jack, were true friends and were quick to offer assistance whenever we needed them. And then there was Sharon Gordon-Link. Sharon and her family lived in Rocklin, and while she didn't know Shalita as well as many of her friends, she made an effort to regularly check in on the boys and me every couple of months for the first few years, for which I will always be grateful.

I also realized that Shalita had introduced me to an amazing culture, with its food, music, and remarkable people. She gave me an understanding of a distant land and culture I knew little about. The smell of cardamom and cumin, chicken tikka masala and dosas; the powerful drama and silliness of Bollywood movies; the warmth and unbreakable bond of family. In essence, she opened up new worlds to me.

Through her journals Shalita gave me beautiful poetry and prayers, words of caring and passion that still inspire me. Shalita exposed me to the beauty and love of her family and her cultural heritage. Through her life and journaling, she showed me the richness of her faith and a life devoted to seeking God with all her heart, mind and soul. I feel so fortunate to have been loved by her so fully and unconditionally. I will always savor the time we had together and I thank God for bringing us together.

Finally, being with Shalita during her illness also provided me with a new perspective. Her disease opened my eyes with regard to my own health. For many years I had suffered from back pain, stomach trouble, joint pain, and lack of adequate sleep. These health issues weighed on me both physically and emotionally. But thinking back to when Shalita was in the hospital for the last time, I realized that my health was better than I had recognized. I could walk, write, talk, hug my boys, laugh, cry, dance, and so much more. Sure, there were times when the pain was so discouraging that I would wonder how much of it I could take. I still don't have complete answers to my health issues, but I realize now that the troubles I have experienced to date were not as big as the mountain they often seemed to be in my mind. I began to realize that these challenges didn't really matter. These were simply "bumps in the road." Because Shalita died at forty-seven, that experience also has taught me that tomorrow is not guaranteed, for any of us. Her death provided me with a greater appreciation for my own health and life itself.

***

As I reflect on this special woman, I smile. So many things I am reminded of.

Sleeping in late.
Daniel crawling into bed and cuddling with his Mommy—her "little furnace," she would say.
Bundled up on a cold wintery day, nose pink and sniffling.
A flowery teapot with just boiled water, two teacups, and English breakfast tea.
The cookie exchange party with the girls (and plenty of tea) just before Christmas.
Tags from a blouse on the bed from T.J. Maxx; marked down another 30 percent.
Talking on the portable phone to her brother Chris. Laughing, smiling, laughing again.
Arms swinging, eyes creased tightly as she shuffles to the bathroom in the middle of the night.
Reading The Carpenters *book in bed, for the fifth time.*
On the hunt at Christmas time for marzipan at Cost Plus World Market.

Talking on the phone to Linda, or Clare, or Roselene or Stephi or Kim or Eileen or...

Ten p.m. walks around Cameron Ranch neighborhood at night as we mulled over the day.

Storming into the bedroom, red faced, steaming at Dryw's lack of respect. The next day cuddling the eighteen-year-old, six-foot-two Dryw.

Reading The Cat in the Hat *to Daniel. "Read me another story, Mommy."*

Jet lagged, talking at two a.m. in bed at the Paris Hilton.

Laughing wildly in a spontaneous fit at some sarcastic comment I made years ago.

Weeping at the loss of her dad.

Sitting by the living room window in the burgundy chair doing her morning devotion, shooting me dirty looks at the noises I make during her quiet time.

Pulling the blanket off me in the middle of the night. Sticking her cold feet on my legs (under great protest!) to warm them up.

Calling me at work for the fourth time that day. "What time will you be home?"

Relishing peppermint ice cream with Dryw and Daniel.

Sucking on salted half lemon when five months pregnant with Daniel.

Talking with John on the phone. "Ok, P-cats, ok, love you, bye."

Filling up the car with her perfume as we head to church. Giving me the what-for for complaining.

Ranting about how rude a student was and how many young people have no manners.

Explaining how she stayed late at school as a pregnant student unloaded to her about the troubles with her boyfriend and parents.

Getting together with the Sierra College girls, eating out, exchanging gifts.

Turning up the radio when a Beatles song came on, remembering every word and singing her heart out.

Going to the Baskin-Robbins on Granite Drive in Rocklin, running into a former student, again.

Talking with her mom, for the third time that day.

Remembering her saying, "Bill, my Bill, you are the best thing that ever happened to me."

Looking into her sparkling dark brown eyes.

190

At the end of the day, as I take my socks off, she dashes by just to beat me into the shower.
How peaceful she looks asleep and putting my finger next to her lips as she kisses it.

Shalita was my soulmate, and I was hers. Despite the difficulties and hurt we inevitably caused each other, despite the frustration and misunderstandings we experienced at times, we deeply loved each other.

While Shalita wanted desperately to live a long and healthy life—to watch her boys grow, to help her mom, to enjoy our marriage as we grew older, to serve God—she accepted her disease and understood the joy that comes from Christ despite the fear and pain that life sometimes throws at us. In his letter to the church in Philippi, the Apostle Paul talks about the key to his inner happiness and peace:

> For I have learned to be content whatever the circumstances. I know what it is to be in need, and I know what it is to have plenty. I have learned the secret of being content in any and every situation, whether well fed or hungry, whether living in plenty or in want. I can do everything through him who gives me strength. (Philippians 4:11–13)

I think Paul could have also said, "I have learned to be content . . . whether I have a full head of hair, or none at all due to chemotherapy; whether healthy or suffering the effects of tumors growing in my body; whether God gives me forty more years of life or forty more days. *I can do everything through him who gives me strength.*"

It was no coincidence that Shalita had underlined these verses in her Bible. She took to heart Paul's message, and while she continued to pray daily for healing, she knew that regardless of her health and the ultimate outcome, she was secure in Christ and would never stop praising him.

From Shalita's journal

October 27, 2001
And the God of <u>all</u> grace who called you to his eternal glory in Christ, after you suffered a little while, will <u>himself</u> <u>restore</u> you and make you <u>strong</u>, <u>firm</u> and <u>steadfast.</u>
- 1 Peter 5:10

Lord Jesus I praise you and bless you today. You alone know how deeply I need you and you alone to <u>restore me</u>. I have suffered and been challenged, worn down and depleted this past year and Father, I need total and complete restoration of my body, mind, heart and soul. Jesus, please heal the deepest hurts, insecurities and anger in me. Please heal my fears and anxieties about the future. I need an infilling and outpouring of your Holy Spirit. Jesus, you have been so good to me. You have answered my prayers and carried me when I have been too weak to pray. You have heard the innermost groanings of my spirit when all I could pray was "Oh Jesus, please help me." Jesus, thy Lord and Savior, I long to be a strong woman of God – a prayer warrior. I have such a sense of my own mortality. What am I leaving behind? What mark will my life make? Will your kingdom be furthered because of me? Jesus, I see so much that I need to do – more lives to touch – starting with my own family, my husband and boys who I love more than my own life. Please give me wisdom and patience and understanding. Help our family be close and a powerful witness for you.

Lord, I pray that you will make me <u>strong</u>, <u>firm</u> and steadfast. My body is so weak and worn out and I ask you please to heal me. I pray for strength to meet all my responsibilities of being a wife, mom, daughter, sister, friend, teacher and homemaker. Please help me to be firm and steadfast in my faith with no compromises. Keep me on an even keel. I struggle with highs and lows emotionally, Lord – I pray that during my lows you would help me cling to the steadfastness of your promises… I pray for all my family, friends – For Dad and Mom, my precious parents – give them a long, happy and healthy life –

Chris, Deb, Christine and Eric, John and Deana, David and Jonathan, Brian, Lori, Susan and the kids, Mom and Dad B – Protect and bless them. Jesus, I give the future to you... Be with my Daniel who lights up my life and along with Dryw is the joy of my heart. Protect him and may he always love you above all else. Father I give my beloved Bill to you – the man of my dreams, my husband and soulmate. Deepen our love, commitment and bless our marriage. Please give us wisdom as parents to listen and seek to understand . . . Please help me be excellent in teaching and wise and compassionate with my students.

Father, it is so good to lay my heart open before you. Thank you for always being here for me – <u>always</u> loving, <u>always</u> being faithful. Please bless me today and make me a blessing. I adore and worship you and love you with my whole heart.

<u>Amen</u>

While Shalita didn't always feel as though she had impacted people's lives, clearly she did. As a teacher she influenced thousands of students, listened to their problems, and provided guidance when asked. Her warm, confident personality and unique ability to connect with people brought many friends in her life. And with her family she maintained a closeness and loyalty that is exceptionally uncommon. As a mother to Dryw and Daniel, she was their biggest supporter and a warm and loving mom. Her constant prayers, support, and love as they grew up will continue to guide them throughout their lives. As a wife, Shalita gave her best during our twelve and a half years of marriage. I always felt her support in my many endeavors, even when my ideas were silly or impractical. She was a most remarkable woman.

***

About a year and a half after Shalita died, I had a dream about her. I was standing next to a river. There were people near me, but I didn't recognize them. Across the deep and wide river I could hear a faint voice. As I strained to listen, I realized it was Shalita, and she was saying something to me. I could see her waving at me. I was so happy to see her. We called out to each other across the divide. "I love you, Shalita!" I yelled to her. "I love you Bill!" she yelled back. While I felt frustrated that the river prevented us from seeing each other up close, from embracing, I was thrilled to see her and communicate with her, even at the great distance.

When I woke up, I realized that the dream was a message. The river represented the gap between the world I lived in and the heavenly realm where Shalita now resides. Although I couldn't touch her or see her up close, her memories were very much a part of me and we could communicate, if in a different way and place.

The dream was a gift from God. I will always cherish it.

Shalita's Prayer

Thou didst give me a song in my heart.
I cannot still the voice from my lips.
How I love you – my incomprehensible living God.
The sound of water lapping against the still bank, propelled by the breeze.
The crests of waves rising higher and higher.
Their creamy frothiness reflected in the hue of the clouds overhead.
They dash against the edge and diminish.
Only to start again – as a ripple, forming into a wave.
The lines and curves of the trees – the hills ahead
Etched so clearly against the blue horizon
No music is sweeter than the sound of Thy creation oh Lord
The sound of waves – the stillness,
Climbing into a lap and then quieting
The sound of the breeze – rippling through every part of me –
or caressing and embracing me in its wake
Till I am caught up totally with it.
No painter could have designed this beauty
Nor a human mind compose such a perfect synchrony of music.
Nor could one produce this aroma of wind, water, grass and nature
Only you could and you have
Thank you for making me a part of this glorious creation
It soothes me
Your creation magnifies you so totally and completely.
The handiwork of your mastermind is truly perfect
I reach out with fingers of faith to you
Through your perfect creation of which I am so insignificant a part
And yet so significant
The labyrinths of my mind cannot grasp the fact of my significance in this galaxy of endless time and space.
What am I? A human being created by you – A woman –
whom you have chosen to shower your love on
What have I done to deserve you?
Why do you love me so deeply with a profundity and intensity that shakes and almost frightens me?
What did I do to be counted worthy of being so whole?

My body, so complex, so delicate – you've designed its synchrony so beautifully
My mind, no, not my body and mind but Thine for I have no claim on them.
I would give them to you – heart, mind, body, intellect, emotion, will – my entire personality for you to work in and through.
Let not a single particle of me be untouched by you
Yes, I'm weak – sinful, broken and yet I am important to you. Only you can make this miracle of grace possible. I love you Lord – all of me is you.
Take me now.

Ajwa Lake (Baroda)
January 18, 1981

196

Family Photographs

Shalita, 1970

Shalita with her parents, 1978

The Chitambar family (left to right): John, Shalita, Ben, Deb, Thea and Chris near their home in Allahabad, India, 1975

Shalita, Daniel, Dryw and Bill, San Diego, 2005

Shalita and Bill at the Louvre, Paris, 2003

About the Author

Bill Blackburn recently retired after working for thirty-three years in the interpretive and environmental fields with the State of California. He lives in Carmichael, California, with his son Daniel and Siberian Husky, Argo.

Made in the USA
San Bernardino, CA
06 July 2018